Fantasy Feast 2000

Thank you

Fantasy Feast 2000 simply could not have been produced without the willing help, advice, time and money of numerous people and organisations.

Pictures & Images

Most of the pictures used in this book were kindly supplied by the following picture libraries:

• Famous Pictures • Alpha Pictures • Illustrated London News Pictures • The Mary Evans Picture Library

Donations

Thanks to the generosity of the following:

• Cazenove & Co • Hello! Magazine • Byron Business Services

Partners, Advisors & Friends

Some advice sticks, no matter how daft you are. More than anyone, these people are responsible for keeping the project alive during our many dark days...

• The Proud Family: Mum, Dad, Alex, Chris, Lorraine, Celia, Anthony, William & Emily. Not quite a mafia yet, but getting there.

• Annie Kirkpatrick: my business partner and then my friend. It's because of you that this has happened. You really do deserve as much credit for this book as I do.

• Bitta Stockton: thanks for all the advice and the many coffee mornings.

• Eleanor Darley, Benedicta Nakawuki and Alan Hodgson: for long hours, late nights and generally sweating it out with me and putting up with my omelette obsession.

• Johnny, Montu, Jim, Josh, Sean & Alex: I'm sorry for being such an ordeal of a flatmate. From now on, I'll be letting go of the evil thoughts and walking to the light. Thanks for all the counselling!

• Marjorie Thompson at Saatchi & Saatchi Cause Connection, Conran Holdings, Freud Communications & Lord Archer: for some gold plated advice from the big boys!

• Save the Children: the most professional charity I've ever worked with. Thanks Sel!

• The Media Fund: I know I'm your worst client Piers, but the book will look pretty on your bookshelf. (And thanks to Charles Hodgson for introducing us!)

The Contributors

Clearly, without your help, we wouldn't have anything to put in the book. The biggest thanks go to you for devoting your time and imagination to create your Fantasy Feasts.

There have been many more people involved in this project whom I will thank at the back of the book, not because they deserve less thanks, but because I cannot thank them all here.

Hector Proud

This book is published by David Campbell publishers Ltd, under one of its imprint, Adelphi.
David Campbell publishers Ltd, Gloucester Mansions, 140A Shaftesbury Avenue, London WC2H 8HD

Fantasy Feast 2000 © based on an original idea by The Idea Generation Limited. 1999

The moral right of the Author has been asserted.
ISBN 1-84159-000-2

Design by bk design
Scans by The Setting Studio, Newcastle

Printed in the EU by Partenaires Livres

Fantasy Feast, the idea

31st December 1999.
The birth of the new Millennium.
The Friday night of all time.

What are you going to be doing? Where are you going to
celebrate it? Who will you be with? These have been *the*
questions of 1999.

But... what if you could hold the ultimate party – a fantasy party –
where anything was possible? What would you do if you could
hold your own Fantasy Feast? Imagine...

...Your Guest List   ANYONE ... from Jesus to John Lennon;
Madonna to Mother Teresa; Homer to Homer Simpson.

...Your Venue   ANYWHERE ... from a deserted Pacific Island
to the foothills of the Andes; from the top of the Empire State
Building to a cosy countryside pub.

...Your Menu & Drink   ANYTHING ... from caviar and
champagne to curry and lager.

...Your Theme   ANY MUSIC... if you had to choose the
soundtrack for the evening, what music would you christen
the next thousand years with?

...Your Toast   ANY REFLECTION... see in the New Millennium
with a toast to the lessons of the past and to hope for the future.

For the past six months, *Fantasy Feast 2000* has approached
hundreds of leading personalities – from the worlds of music, art,
literature, politics, fashion, sport, design, science, film, TV & radio
– and asked them to create their ultimate party. Their Fantasy
Feasts are here for you to see...

The only question that remains is: What would *you* do?

The *Fantasy Feast 2000* concept was developed by
Hector Proud and The Idea Generation Company to raise funds
for Save The Children. All author royalties are being donated to
Save the Children.

Contents

Save the Children

Imagine all the children – safe, healthy, well fed, educated, happy. What a world it would be. This is Save the Children's goal – not a crazy dream – to create a world where all children have everything they need to thrive and grow. If all children had this, chances are they'd make a better world for future generations.

We are the UK's leading international children's charity working in over 65 countries in the world. In a world where children are denied basic human rights, we champion the right to a happy, healthy and secure childhood.

Emergency relief runs alongside long-term development and prevention work to help children, their families and communities to be self-sufficient. We involve children in all our work – we believe in listening to and learning from them and put them at the heart of everything we do.

Some of our achievements to-date include:

• Developing a travelling nursery education service to give rural children in the UK a chance to learn.

• Successfully reuniting over 5,000 families torn apart by war in Rwanda.

• Supporting night schools for 2,500 working children in Rajasthan, India.

• Distributing medicines, food and surgical materials to 300 health units in Cuba.

• Providing support to half a million children in Iraqi Kurdistan through community services, advocacy and education.

• Establishing a telephone service enabling family members having been separated by the conflict in Kosovo to keep in touch – over 1,000 calls were placed each day during the heart of the crisis.

All author royalties from the sale of this book are being donated to Save the Children to help us, and the children we work with, to build a better world for present and future generations.

If you would like more information on Save the Children or if you or your company would like to help us, either by making a donation or volunteering your time, please contact us on 0171 703 5400 or check out our web-site at www.savethechildren.org.uk. Alternatively you can write to us at 17 Grove Lane, London, SE5 8RD.

As President of Save the Children, I am delighted that so many busy, well-known people have taken the time to contribute to this book. As we enter the 21st Century, it is fitting to commemorate this historic event but vital that, fantasies aside, we remember and act on behalf of all those for whom a change of date does not mean a change of circumstances.

All around the world there are children who do not have the kind of childhood that many of us have enjoyed. Millions of children do not have access to clean, safe water, regular education, or a healthy diet. Hundreds of thousands of children around the world are fighting in, or affected by, adults' wars.

It is easy to feel there is little any one person can do, but in fact the good news is that there are many people around the world who are committed to making a difference.

The sale of this book will help to raise money for Save the Children which, for over 80 years, has been supporting children in some of the poorest communities across the world. The Fund's aim is to give every child the happy, healthy and secure childhood that will help them to become successful and responsible adults whatever their race, nationality, or creed. The money raised by all those who buy this book will help make this possible. Thank you all, for your support.

Anne

Her Royal Highness, The Princess Royal,
President of Save the Children

...No, you bring a bottle like every other guest

Sewell.

911

A1

guests Robbie Williams, all our mates, and all our families.

location
Lee: In Carlisle United's football ground.
Spike: In Warrington, near Mr. Smith's!

menu A few beers!

music Robbie's album – it's cool!

toast Hooray, hooray, Millennium, Millennium!

guests We'd invite everyone in the world if it was the ultimate party... and everyone in the universe and other galaxies – let's have a huge inter-galactic party.

location In Ben's front room – could you image the whole world in his front room – it'd be excellent!

menu Loadsa champagne and wine – anything anyone wanted would be there!

music We all like different music so it would be a bit of everything... rock, pop, R&B, soul. We'd have a huge jukebox with thousands of wicked tunes on it!

toast Here's to a brilliant year and an even better one to come. Cheers! Be the first to believe!

Robbie Williams

let's have a
huge
inter-galactic
party

All Saints

Natalie Appleton

guests Stephen King I love his novels, and I'd ask him where he gets his ideas from and find out what makes him tick.

Nicky Appleton We're always together and it wouldn't be the same without her. She's really good fun as well.

Gene Simmons and Paul Stanley I'm a huge Kiss fan and I would love to have these two at my party.

LilyElla Melanie's daughter.

Dave Grohl (Foo Fighters) I was a huge fan of Nirvana, and now of Foo Fighter as well.

Gary Oldman A truly charismatic and very talented actor. I'd like him to be there as I like to be surrounded by people I respect.

Brad Pitt Again, I'm a big fan, and, of course, it's always nice to have good looking men at your party.

Helene Blatt Melanie's mother.

David Moores (management's assistant) Simply because he always looks after me and I wouldn't worry about anything if he was there.

Snuffleupagus (from *Sesame Street*) The children would have to have someone for them, and I always used to love *Sesame Street*, so it would be as much fun for me!

Sesame Street

Brad Pitt

location In my own home, with my daughter Rachel – a really warm, friendly, relaxed environment.

menu As it's a special celebration, lots of good champagne, obviously, and tequila to really get the party going.

seating plan I really don't like seating plans because a party means you should get the chance to talk to everyone – so at my party I'd like everyone to swap seats after each course.

music All Saints, obviously.

toast I would ask everyone to raise their glasses and toast their families, their friends, and all the things we have to be grateful for. I don't much go for big slushy speeches, but the Millennium New Year has to be a time for a certain amount of reflection and gratitude for the nice things we have. Also a time to look forward to all the exciting things that could happen in the new Millennium.

Shami Ahmed (Joe Bloggs)

I launched Joe Bloggs Jeans when I was just 24 years old. As a teenager, Bloggs was just a dream and today it is a multi-million pound business, operating internationally and providing me with an opportunity to fulfil my other ambitions.

guests Sameena Ahmed (my wife)
Entertainment, music and good fun will be phenomenal with the combination of these names:
Frank Sinatra
Elvis Presley
Jimi Hendrix
Nushkat Fateh Ali Khan
David Bowie
Celine Dion
Eddie Murphy and Jim Carey
For comedy and laughter.
Stanley Kubrick and Alfred Hitchcock
For fascinating conversation, and I would ask them to make a film of the evenings' celebrations.

location The Taj Mahal – a beautiful setting for what will be a momentous occasion.

menu An assortment of traditional curries and champagne – essential for toasting in the New Year.

music With the guest list highlighted we will make our own music – the combination will be phenomenal.

toast In some ways, a new Millennium provides a new start; an opportunity for us all to better the world we live in and to create opportunities for generations to come.

David Bowie

11

Ant & Dec
Declan Donnelly

I spent five years in the children's soap *Byker Grove*. Went on to have a music career, made 3 albums and I'm now hosting ITV's Saturday morning offering SMTV LIVE, made by my production company 'Ant and Dec Productions Ltd.'

guests Elvis To give us a little song. Kevin Keegan To talk footy. Kylie Minogue To drool over! Roald Dahl To tell us some *Tales of the Unexpected*! Rod Serling, creator of *The Twilight Zone* To try to outdo Roald Dahl so we would all benefit from their competitive story telling! Eddie Izzard To laugh at. Ant McPartlin He's me pal, isn't he? Harry Houdini To do magic. Basil Brush 'Cos I like him. Boom, Boom! Jackie Milburn Old Newcastle United player who could tell us about when Newcastle actually won stuff!!

location A Penthouse loft on Newcastle's quayside, overlooking the River Tyne and the Tyne Bridge.

menu A nice Sauvignon Blanc and McEwans lager (and some Asti Spumanti for the lasses!) The menu would be a huge Chinese banquet, starting with mixed hors d'oeuvres, crispy aromatic duck, and then lots of popular dishes.

seating plan I'm not really bothered where everyone sits as long as I'm near the lasses (and the footballers)!

toast Raise your glasses ladies and gentlemen – that was a good 'un, let's make this one better!

Eddie Izzard

Basil Brush

Another Level
Mark Baron

I enjoy company, I enjoy people, I like having fun, I'm creative – I'm just a fun person to be with! (I don't like mornings!)

Ant & Dec
Anthony McPartlin

At thirteen I started acting in *Byker Grove*. Since then I've gone on to have 3 albums and a great pop career. Now I'm enjoying a fantastic career as a TV presenter. I'm a very happy and lucky little Geordie!

guests Kevin Keegan To talk about football all night, and also ask him to come back to Newcastle.
The Corrs Because they're gorgeous! They could play us into the Millennium.
Lots of Playboy Bunnies Need I say more?
John Lennon He was just fantastic.
Jarvis Cocker He's such a character. A great bloke to sit and chat to.

Vic and Bob To make us laugh all night.
A top magician Every party needs one.
Cat and Dec 'Cos they're my mates.
Alex Garland He's the author of *The Beach*, which is one of my favourite novels. He can tell us stories.
Jack Nicholson He's my favourite actor and such a dude.
Bertie Bassett He'd be the first to be eaten when we run out of food.

location A remote island just off the east coast of Australia.

menu Everything has to be savoury – crisps, nuts, scotch eggs, sausage rolls – and mince pies from Greggs the bakers. White wine (Jacob's Creek or Coldstream Hills), lots of lager, Guinness, white rum and Coke.

seating plan I would sit next to all the foxy chicks and all the good looking blokes would sit at the back in the shade.

music The Beatles, Oasis, the Doors, Blur, Pulp, Burt Bacharach, the Cuban All Stars, the Cure, Air, Massive Attack.

Jack Nicholson

John Lennon

guests Stevie Wonder I've always been a big fan and would like to talk to him.
Neil Armstrong I'd like to talk to him and find out about his life's experiences.
Lee Evans I think he's absolutely hilarious.
Both grandfathers One I never met, and neither did my father; the other died when I was five and I'd like to talk to him as I don't remember him that well.
Jennifer Lopez
Homer Simpson I'm a big fan, but only as long he didn't eat all the food.
Winston Churchill My dad has always collected loads of stuff about him. He's just a dominant figure and would be head of the table.

The Welsh guy from *Notting Hill* (Rhys Ifans) I met him at a dinner party and he's absolutely hilarious. That's *him* in the film; he's not acting, that's just how he is. Mad! One of the funniest people I've ever met.
Ian Wright I've met him and we got on really well.
Mike Read I haven't met him, but I've got his videos and I find him really funny.
James Dean My nickname!

location On a private yacht in a prime position to watch the Monaco Grand Prix.

menu Oysters, lobsters – I'm a big fan of seafood, and champagne.

seating plan Winston Churchill at the head of the table, Mike Read and Lee Evans on either side of me, and everyone else could just mingle and go where they like.

music A mixture of classic stuff like Otis Reading, Stevie Wonder and Lionel Ritchie, with more up-to-date stuff towards the later part of the evening – some good dance tracks.

toast Let's make the next 2,000 years less traumatic than the last 2,000.

Steven Appleby

I'm a cartoonist and an artist. Too much of the time I live in invented versions of the real world (but inside my head). I draw for *The Guardian*, *The Times* and *The Telegraph*; I create books for Bloomsbury Publishing, and animated series for T.V.

guests **My mother** Ibbie Appleby. **My father** Walter Appleby. My parents are both dead (in 1981 and 1993) and it would be lovely to see them again, and for them to meet my wife.

Nicola My wife. Nicola hasn't met my parents – she's also a wonderful conversationalist and would get the best out of everyone!

Fats Waller Dad's favourite piano player and singer. Fats could play for us all.

Bing Crosby Mum's favourite singer – he could join Fats on the piano.

Harpo Marx Reputed to be a wonderful person. I (and mum and dad) would enjoy hearing him talk.

Philip K. Dick Science fiction writer and visionary: a big influence on me. Mad.

Houdini Magic would be a good entertaining thing for after dinner. Maybe he'd have met all the others in the afterlife.

Edward Gorey My favourite living artist/author/gothic strange world inventor.

Matt Groening Inventor of the astonishing *The Simpsons*.

Ru Paul And finally, a touch of other-worldly glamour.

location The house I grew up in – an old vicarage – in the condition it was in when we lived there. Sold after my mum died, it is now an old people's home.

menu Christmas dinner, with all the trimmings, including crackers, hats and indoor fireworks. A good three to four hour over-the-top stuffing. Not forgetting, for pudding, Grannie's Goo – a whipped cream and marshmallow experience – not to everyone's taste.

music Fats Waller, Bing Crosby, Harpo Marx and all the others joining in.

toast "To the world, and all the people passing through."

Houdini

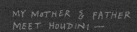

MY MOTHER & FATHER MEET HOUDINI —

Happy New Year!

HARPO ASKS FOR SECONDS OF TURKEY —

TOOT TOOT TOOT

Ibbie and Walter Appleby

too much of the time
I live in invented versions
of the real world

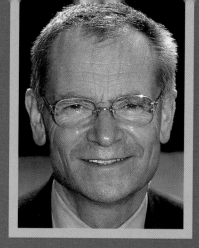

Jeffrey Archer

Married to Mary, 2 sons, Will and James. Author of 10 books, 3 sets of short stories, and 2 plays; published in 64 countries, with international sales of more than 120 million. Former MP and Deputy Chairman of the Conservative Party. Made a Life Peer in Queen's Birthday Honours List, 1992.

Thomas Jefferson

Nelson Mandela

Benjamin Disraeli

Elisabeth the First

guests

Thomas Jefferson

William Shakespeare

Muhammad Ali

Benjamin Franklin

Nelson Mandela

Elizabeth I

Donald Bradman

Benjamin Disraeli

Catherine the Great

Frank Sinatra

Mary Archer

location My house in London, overlooking the Thames.

menu A fish soup • Shepherd's pie • Raspberry sorbet • Cheddar cheese • Champagne (Krug)

music Frank Sinatra, Mozart, Sammy Davis Jr, The Beatles, Louis Armstrong.

toast To an end to prejudices of all kinds.

seating plan

Benjamin Disraeli — Shakespeare — Mary Archer — Benjamin Franklin — Donald Bradman — Nelson Mandela — Thomas Jefferson — Jeffrey Archer — Elizabeth the First — Catherine the Great — Frank Sinatra — Muhammad Ali

Paddy Ashdown

I never, ever, describe myself!

guests

Firstly, my close family My wife Jane, son Simon, and daughter Kate and her family.

Lao Tse Chinese philosopher from 6th-century BC. For a chance to listen to his spiritual and moral wisdom.

Alexander the Great Soldier-king, conqueror of Persia. To witness his unparalleled energy, courage and leadership.

King Arthur Britain's most celebrated monarch. Because I'm from the West Country!

Marco Polo Venetian merchant explorer. To listen to his vast wealth of travelling tales.

John Donne Metaphysical poet and priest. To add colour and wit to the conversation.

J. M. W. Turner 18th-century landscape painter. For his insight and vision.

Charles James Fox 19th-century British Whig statesman. To experience some of his passionate oratory.

Sir Ernest Henry Shackleton Antarctic explorer. To hear how it felt to tread where no one had ever been.

Mahatma Gandhi The spiritual leader of Indian Independence I was born in India so Gandhi's been a lifelong inspiration.

Don Giovanni Mozart's operatic hero. To liven up the party and to sing in the Millennium!

menu

What I think would be most enjoyable is just some simple home French cooking; several courses which linger for a good few hours – including a fish course and a decent cut of fresh lamb, plenty of bread, and as many varieties of the local wine as the guests would wish to drink.

location

Our small family cottage in Irancy – a rural village in the heart of the Burgundy region of France.

seating plan

Guests, obviously, would be free to sit as they wish, but my suggestion would be seating them according to historical seniority – Lao Tse at the head, and my grandson, Matthais next to me at the other end.

Tasmin Archer

British soul singer Tasmin Archer's silky voice on her debut album *Great Expectations* and hit single *Sleeping Satellite* propelled her to stardom in 1993.

Lao Tse

Sir Ernest Shackleton (right) with Robert Peary

toast To quote T.E. Lawrence: 'All men dream, but not equally. Those who dream by night in the dusty recesses of their minds, wake in the morning to find it was vanity: but dreamers of the day are dangerous men, for they act their dream with open eyes, to make it possible.'

So my toast is to men and women that have, through the ages, been willing to dream, not just for themselves, but for society, their families, their communities and their nations.

I would also like to toast those dreamers willing to set their faces towards a different kind of world in the next Millennium.

One in which each person's potential is realised, each person's contribution is valued, each person's vote counts, each person's rights are enshrined in law. In which each person recognises their dependence on others, not just within their own country or community, but in the world which belongs to us all.

guests
The table is round. I am at 12 o'clock and clockwise the seating plan is:

Me
Bob Dylan
Alice Walker
Gary Cooper
Maya Angelou
Jiddu Krishnamurti
Bjork
John Hughes
Mary Shelley
Jimi Hendrix
Ella Fitzgerald
Seymour Benzer

location
The site of the clock of the Long Now if it is decided by then, or failing that, Stonehenge.

music
Rubber Soul – The Beatles.
The Koln Concert – Keith Jarrett.
Pet Sounds – The Beach Boys.
Palm Tree – Superstar.
Blue – Joni Mitchell.
Hello Nasty – The Beastie Boys.

menu
British fish-shop fish and chips wrapped in newspaper with lots of salt and vinegar. Vanilla ice-cream with strawberries. Washed down with that black Irish stuff or mineral water if preferred.

toast The year 2000 is no more than a landmark – let's not make it a barrier. Let us move forward together as one, living in the present, accepting the past, and looking to the future with an open mind and heart.

Naim Attallah

Self-made man of modest and varied achievements. Lover of the arts and the good things in life. Blue-collar worker in early days, rising to foreign exchange dealer, banker, impresario, film producer, journalist, publisher and one-time group chief executive of Asprey plc.

goodbye to religious intolerance, political correctness, ball-breaking women and man's inhumanity to man

guests   Julian of Norwich Because of her assurance that everything is held in being by the love of God, so that ' all will be well'.

Simone de Beauvoir A genuine feminist, a pioneer and an example to women – more interesting than her lover, Jean Paul-Sartre.

Diana Mosley For telling the truth in the face of constant vilification.

Santa Sebag Montefiore For her loveliness and charm.

Cristina Odone A woman 'of the faith' with a combination of northern poise and Mediterranean ardour.

Helen Mirren The doyenne of intelligent acting.

Sylvie Guillem For her exquisite ballet dancing.

Jacqueline Du Pre To provide the music.

My grandmother For her beauty of spirit and wisdom.

Maya Angelou A beautiful black singer, poet and writer who has triumphed over adversity and shown that love conquers all.

Anais Nin She would inflame the after-dinner conversation with an account of her erotic voyage of self-discovery.

location   'La Guillarmie' would be the venue. It is the name of my house in the Dordogne, set on a hillside in the rolling countryside, which is forever changing colour and shifting shape. Montaigne, the Dordogne's famous son, wrote, "To live properly is our great and glorious masterpiece! When you travel to the Dordogne, the masterpiece is glimpsed, and once glimpsed it is never forgotten.

menu   Pink tomatoes with olive oil, balsamic vinegar and basil (each tomato weighing more than one pound, from the market at Siorac in the Dordogne);
Magret de canard (a local speciality, cooked rare and beautifully tender);
Crêpes flambées;
Cheval blanc 1947.

seating plan   My dinner guests are a mixture of the spiritual, the erotic, and the pioneering, with levels of passion and beauty equally distributed. The choice of seating can therefore be left to them.

music

Allegri's Miserere.
Rachmaninoff: Piano Concerto N0.1 (F-sharp minor).
Schubert: Piano Trio (B-flat major).
Wagner: The Siegfried Idyll.
Bach: Goldberg Variations.

toast   Toast goodbye to religious intolerance, political correctness, ball-breaking women and man's inhumanity to man. In the Millennium I propose a toast to the peace makers, especially those who are working to bring about a lasting settlement in the Middle East. To a new cultural enlightenment, including an enhanced Royal Opera House.

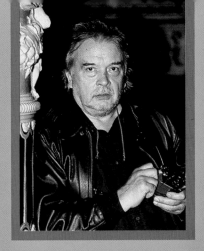

David Bailey

Born in London in 1938, David Bailey originally specialised in fashion photography. His creative approach soon extended to portraits expressing the spirit of the Swinging Sixties and to some outstanding studies of the nude.

guests

Picasso Greatest 20th-century artist.
Buddha Universal good.
Orson Welles To keep the conversation going.
Louis Armstrong Invented popular music.
Charles Darwin To put it all into perspective.
Cleopatra The first feminist.

Merlin To keep up the fantasy.
Venus She might be able to tell me something I've missed.
André Malraux To write a thesis on the dinner.
Baroness Blixen Written the greatest book by any woman.
Catherine Bailey Because she is the most important person in the world to me.

location

A house-boat in Kashmir.

menu

Food would have to be vegetarian because of Buddha. Good wine.

seating plan

The guests would find their own order.

Louis Armstrong

Pablo Picasso

Hope the next one is better than the last one

Ronnie Barker

I was lucky enough to have a very successful career as a comedian, and drew great satisfaction from this and from the happiness derived from the love of a wonderful woman and a delightful family.

Danny Kaye

Dorothy Parker

Orson Welles

guests

Charles Dickens For conversation.
Ingrid Bergman For beauty.
Danny Kaye For warmth.
Marilyn Monroe For fun.
Laurence Olivier For charm.
My wife, Joy For love.
Eric Morecambe For entertainment.
Elizabeth I For greatness.
Dorothy Parker For wit.
Orson Welles For charisma.
Toulouse-Lautrec For nostalgia.

location

The Hotel Regina Europa overlooking the Grand Canal in Venice - because of the sunset and, later, the lights on the gondolas reflected in the water and the serenading of the gondolieri.

menu

Chilli con carne; Italian ice-cream; Dom Perignon champagne.

music

Simon and Garfunkel and The Beatles; the folk music of the late 20th century, when songs had a melody...

toast

May the mistakes made in the last century be absent in this new one.

seating plan

Round table – Ronnie Barker at 12 o'clock then clockwise: Laurence Olivier, Joy Barker, Danny Kaye, Marilyn Monroe, Orson Welles, Dorothy Parker, Elizabeth I, Eric Morecambe, Charles Dickens, Toulouse-Lautrec, Ingrid Bergman. Reason for this seating – they would each have someone wonderful to talk to!

Generous, considerate and vulnerable. I have managed in my life to make millions of people smile and, for a short while, forget their problems, and they have helped me to achieve self-dignity.

Michael Barrymore

Jack Nicholson

Princess Diana

Joanna Lumley

Oprah Winfrey

guests

Jack Nicholson Best actor in the world.

Princess Diana For befriending me in a time of need.

Toad of Toad Hall Because I was him in a former life.

Steve Martin My favourite comedian.

Cruella de Ville To make everybody else on the table look nice.

Muhammad Ali So no one else on the table can be the greatest.

My mum to confuse everybody at the table with her logic.

Joanna Lumley (a.k.a Patsy) To make sure all the booze is used up.

Jennifer Saunders My favourite comedienne.

Oprah Winfrey To organise all the arguments.

Batman My favourite childhood hero.

location The classic yacht Rosenkavalier (built 1929 by Krupp in Germany), moored in Monaco. Reason: elegance abounds.

menu Steamed artichokes and asparagus with herb mayonnaise. Roasted game hens with wild rice stuffing, tandoori parsnips, peppered flour roasted potatoes, mushroom medley and fried onion in gravy. Dark chocolate bombe filled with Grand-Marnier ice-cream. Tequila, Sambuca, wines and spirits chosen by the head wine waiter of the Lanesborough Hotel, London.

seating plan Every half an hour the music will start and stop, everyone gets up and walks around the table and sits when the music stops.

music The Boxer by Simon and Garfunkel.

toast To the apple, more precisely the apple turnover, Eve turned over an apple to Adam. More than once in anyone's life they promise to turn over a new leaf. Winter turns over its harshness to spring, after wars prisoners are turned over to their loved ones. Evil men have turned over the poor and vulnerable. The young turn over their trust in anyone. Anyone can turn over in bed, except those with a nurse by their side. In my life I've turned over a page only to see that the script gets worse! Industry lives by its turnover. Farmers bring us fresh food when they turnover the soil. When your turn's over in a game you always wonder if you could have made a better move. So when the game of life is over, it's for us to turnover – to the future. P.T.O. The Apple.

Basil Brush

I made animal TV presenters acceptable and paved the way for the likes of Kermit the frog, Miss Piggy, Roland the Rat, Noel Edmonds etc... I also believe that through my show people came to realise just how interesting, intelligent and funny foxes can be. This, I'm sure, started the anti-fox hunting movement.

David Attenborough So interesting and polite, and so good with animals

David Attenborough

guests Basil Fawlty For his excellent choice of name and world famous organisational skills. He can help arrange the dinner and bring Manuel to help with the drinks.

Lord Charles Nice to have some blue blood on the table, aristocratic style. Also, we share the same profession, we speak while some dummy makes our mouths move. Boom! Boom!

Samantha Fox Obviously a distant relative.

Lamb Chop Again a professional interest, and because it's nice to see some lamb at the dinner table...

Guy Fawkes He was involved in the gunpowder plot, you know – Boom! Boom! Interested to hear his political views and who better to arrange the fireworks?

David Attenborough So interesting and polite, and so good with animals.

James Herriot You cannot leave out the family doctor, can you?

Mr. Derek Co-presenter and friend for so many years. He can read the bed-time story...I won't interrupt, you know.

Colonel Sanders Excellent chicken snacks – my favourite.

Terry Thomas Great British actor who, in my early career, I modelled myself on! We also have the same teeth.

Michael J. Fox He can bring a bit of Hollywood to the evening...I'm sure we must be related?

location The Millennium Dome...someone's got to use it!!

menu Jelly babies, bangers and mash for main course, with gob-stoppers and ice-cream for pud... washed down with loads of Poky Pola, then coffee with Fox's Glacier Mints.

music Abba's greatest hits! They were on my show you know. And of course, the fox-trot.

toast

There was a young fox called Basil,
Who went out one night on the razzle,
He had too much to drink,
Kissed a lady in mink,
And got thrown out by his ears for the hassle.
Boom! Boom!

Brilliant, handsome, a genius, shy. Achievements cover more than 50 words ...fibber.

George Best

to the politicians...

Rod Stewart

Elizabeth Taylor

Sir Winston Churchill

Brigitte Bardot

guests

Oscar Wilde Wit.

Lord Lucan Reward.

Denis Law Laughter.

Sophia Loren Beauty.

Rod Stewart Football.

Sir Winston Churchill To have a drink with him.

Elizabeth Taylor Beauty and class.

Cassius Clay The greatest.

Mary Peters The good and wonderful side of Ulster.

Brigitte Bardot The original beauty.

Richard Burton To see who he'd pull.

location The Oyster Bar in Harrods
(the chairman's paying).

menu Lobster, crab, prawns.
Black Velvet

seating plan First to arrive sits
down first.

music The Three Tenors.

toast To the politicians – stop
talking and start acting.
For the new Millennium – total peace for the 99% of real people in northern Ireland.

Oscar Wilde O · O NAYLOR

Betty Boop

guests Ooooh, what a WONDERFUL idea to have a party for the turn of the century! I just ADORE parties 'cause they're so much FUN! Let's see... here's who I'd invite:

My uncle, Max Fleischer 'Cause he was a brilliant animator, a real pioneer in the field and an absolute genius. After all, he created me! He invented the rotoscope, which allowed him to give me the same kind of realistic movement as my real-life co-stars in the cartoons – great entertainers such as Louis Armstrong, Cab Calloway, Maurice Chevalier and Ethel Merman. Uncle Max brought me out of the inkwell and helped guide me to fame and fortune. And I've been a star ever since!

Bimbo 'Cause before I got into the act, he was the big star of Uncle Max's cartoon films for Paramount – the first animated 'talkies'. In fact, Bimbo played in my very first movie, and, after all these years, he's still my best friend.

Pudgy Naturally – because he's my ever-faithful pooch and constant companion. I love him, even if he does get into hilarious jams· all the time!

Mae Questel 'Cause she provided my distinctive 'Boop-Ooop-a-Doop' voice in Uncle Max's cartoons.

Marilyn Monroe and Madonna I guess you could say I was the first – the original sex symbol. Marilyn and Madonna have made the best of their glamorous, sensuous images too, and they'll always be stars – just like me!

Gabrielle Chanel Even though she borrowed the idea from me, mon amie Coco is credited with designing the little black dress; so simple, so elegant, a little black dress makes every woman look like the star she is!

Anton Kliegl and his brother, John Kliegl (the inventors of Klieg lights) After all, how would anyone be able to see me if those big, bright Kliegs weren't lighting me up!

William Shakespeare 'Cause he wrote the most beautiful sonnets and plays about a subject dear to my heart – love!

Saint Valentine 'Cause Valentine's Day reminds us all that love makes the world go round!

location The world's biggest TV studio.

menu Chocolates, 'cause they're naughty, but oh so Boopalicious!

music I Wanna Be Loved By You, 'cause love is a many splendoured thing.

Madonna

Gabrielle Chanel

Marilyn Monroe

Chocolates, 'cause they're naughty, but oh so Boopalicious!

I am a woman leader born in a traditional society who overcame patriarchal domination and a military dictatorship. Although tragedy walked hand in hand with triumph, I never gave up believing that the love and support of the people of Pakistan had put me in a special place, at a special time, to make a difference.

Benazir Bhutto

My Fantasy Feast shall be a feast only for women. The third Millennium will see an increasing number of females take up positions of power and influence. We will gather to toast the success of women in overcoming obstacles to carve out a place of honour, dignity and equality for themselves in the world at large.

guest **Eve** Who started it all when she asked Adam to get her the apple. After the fall from Paradise, men punished women but women began fighting back, refusing to accept male domination. As the years passed, the battle for equal rights and opportunity began triumphing.

Baroness Margaret Thatcher [*host*] The first woman to be elected prime minister of Great Britain. She changed the course of world history. Her special relationship with the United States and her inflexible commitment to free market economics unleashed a revolution. That revolution resulted in the fall of the Berlin Wall and the end of the Soviet Union (with it ended the bi-polar world).

Joan of Arc The French maid whose visions spelt victory, torment and religious frenzy.

Elizabeth I The virgin Queen of England, whose reign gave birth to a renaissance.

The Empress Nur Jehan A refugee from the court of the Persian King. She married the Moghul Emperor Jehangir who hunted and socialised while she ruled Hindustan, India. She signed agreements with foreign traders whom she received at the Royal Court.

Dame Freya Stark An explorer born around 1892, she spent her life exploring the Middle East, Arabia, Persia, Kurdistan, Iraq and Syria. She travelled alone, a single woman, into areas so wild and dangerous that no 'white man' would dare to travel there. She learnt the languages, made original research in archaeology, and earned universal respect.

Queen Jinga of Angola She led her people to war against the Portugese, to defend their freedom.

Rabia the Muslim woman sufi A mystic elevated to sainthood, who triumphed over patriarchal barriers in opening the way for achieving sainthood for women in muslim societies.

Valentina Tereshnikova A Russian astronaut who was the first woman to travel out of earth and into space.

Bakhtwar Zardari my daughter
The first child born to a woman premier in office, who went with me in my womb to the Siachen glaciers, proving that little girls can climb the highest and iciest glaciers even before they are born.

Aseefa Zardari Whom I was carrying when I was teargassed and chased by police for five hours in Rawalpindi city, during the Long March for Democracy in November 1992.

menu The banquet table is laid out in cloth embroidered in gold and silver thread, in a silken tent on the banks of the River Indus. It is a clear sparkling night, with a cool breeze blowing. Only pashmina shawls are needed • Drinks: mango juice, coconut juice, pomegranate juice, guava juice, lassi, thadal (an almond juice), rose and motia (a flower) sherbets • Starters: caviar, smoked salmon with wafer thin toast, Palla eggs (an Indus fish) • Main course: Taka Tak, local kidney and liver dish from Lahore, duck in plum sauce, chapli kababs from Peshawer, partridges cooked Sindhi style, roast lamb, or sajji, from Balauchistan, tomato cut from hyderabad daccan, okra cooked in yoghurt and tamarind, brinjal stuffed with yoghurt and fried in herbs, boiled rice, fried rice with peas, chappatis, naan and Jowar Ki Roti, a local bread • For those who are dieting: salade niçoise, chicken and almond salad, Caesar salad with grilled turkey • Dessert: apricots boiled in sugar with cream; Dhuk, an ancient blacksweet from Larkana whose recipe is a jealous secret passed by word of mouth; bhusari, a chapati like sweet cooked with Gur-unrefined sugar lumps-Shahi Tukra with real silver paper on top, a type of local bread pudding; Gajar Ka Halwa, a sweet dish made with carrot and raisins, dried sevian with almonds and raisins (a vermicelli dessert) • Fruit: plums, apples, apricots and pomegranates from Balauchistan • Tea: Pink tea from Kashmir, mint tea, peppermint tea, Illaichis, Saunf and bitter mints for after dinner.

Ms. Bhutto's charity, the Sindh Welfare Trust, promotes education and other charitable works. The Sindh Welfare Trust, Bilawal House, D/30, Block 3, Karachi, Pakistan.

Raymond Blanc

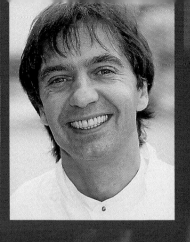

In 1984 I fulfilled a personal vision when I opened Le Manoir aux Quat' Saisons in Great Milton, Oxford. It is the only country house hotel in the UK which has achieved two Michelin stars for a total of 14 years.

Helena Bonham-Carter
because I have always had a strong attraction for her

guests Arthur Rimbaud and Oscar Wilde Rimbaud did not get on too well with his partner and Oscar Wilde might be right for him.

Germaine Greer and Lesbos Lesbos was the first feminist and lesbian. Interesting discussion would follow between the two of them.

Richard Burton and Elizabeth Taylor Most unhappy love affair of the century but maybe they could make up if brought back together.

Napoleon and Josephine He could see how Europe has progressed and crea:te a united Europe. Would be interesting to get to know Josephine.

Helen Bonham Carter and Raymond Blanc I have always had a strong attraction for her.

music Classical: Tomaso Albinoni's six oboe concertos. This piece of music is particularly fluid, evocative and deeply romantic. I have a particular attachment for Albinoni's music.

Jazz/Blues: The Best of Nina Sirnone – a selection of Nina Simone's late 1950's and 1960's songs.

Rock and Pop: the Best of Lionel Richie.

location My 15th-century manor house, Le Manoir aux Quat' Saisons.

menu

Oscar Wilde

Assiette apéritive
Champagne 'Veuve Clicquot'

Fondant de saumon Glenarm et copeaux de morue, salade de mouli et concombres;
sauce au raifort
Confit of Glenarm salmon, flakes of salted cod, mouli and cucumber salad,
horseradish sauce

Vin de Pays du Var 1995
Viognier, Triennes, Domaine de Triennes

Germaine Greer

Risotto au jus de cèpes et verveine, émincé de truffes noires du Périgord, feuilles
d'hiver croustillantes
Risotto with ceps scented with verbena, émincé of Perigold black truffles and crispy
winter leaves

Il Vignola Sauvignon, Avignonesi 1994
Toscana

Gigot de lotte rôti, sauce moutarde et vinaigre; fondue de tomates au jus de viande
Roasted monkfish, tomato fondue; mustard and vinegar sauce

Chablis 1996
Premier Cru Vau Ligneau, Thierry Hamelin

Napoléon by NAYLOR

Pigeonneau 'd'Agen' rôti, son jus et raviole de foie gras, fricassée de girolles et
herbes à soupe
Roasted 'Agen' Squab and foie gras ravioli, fricassée of wild mushrooms

Ribera del Duero 1993
Crianza Cillar de Silos

Petite crème brûlée à la vanille Bourbon
Little crème brûlée scented with Bourbon Vanilla

Maury 1996
Vintage Mas Amiel

Liz Taylor and Richard Burton

Trois petits desserts sur un thème de chocolat
Three little chocolate desserts from Le Manoir

Le Gâteau du Nouvel An

Café 'Pur Arabica', petits fours et chocolats du Manoir

Boy George

guests

Tom Cruise
Archbishop Desmond Tutu
David Beckham
Gerry Adams – I'd like to ask him a few questions.
Charlotte Rampling
David Bowie
The Dalai Lama
Barbara Windsor
Maya Angelou
My mother
My sister, Siobhan

location

If they would allow it, I'd choose my friend's parent's house in Provence but they would have to be invited too as they are the best hosts in the world. Their house is set in 100 acres of land overlooking mountains and valleys. It is absolute heaven.

menu

The food would have to be absolutely vegan. No dead animals, dairy or sugar, but it would be really tasty, I promise. I'd have to bring my friend, Dragona, who is the best macrobiotic cook and the food would be exquisite and cruelty-free – after all, how can you celebrate the Millennium by chomping on veal – urgh!! My friend's parents have their own wine cellar and they know a thing or two about good wines. I'd like them to order it and get Tom Cruise to pay for it.

music

The music would be a mixture of pop and classical, early Bowie, Nina Simone and even a bit of Madonna when people get stupidly drunk.

toast

My toast would be to enter the next Millennium with more love and compassion in our hearts. For governments to stop selling arms and for the whole world to turn vegetarian. I would use my favourite quote from the Dalai Lama; perhaps if we got him drunk enough he might say it himself: 'If you can in this life, help others. If you can't, don't hurt them.'

If you can in this life, help others.
If you can't don't hurt them

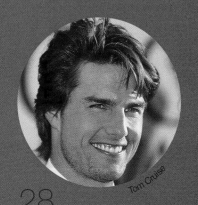

Tom Cruise

Dalai Lama

David Bowie

David Beckham

I am a comic and I hope
I've made people laugh.
I used to be a psychiatric nurse.

Jo Brand

guests

Germaine Greer Quite the most inspired and intelligent woman of our age.

Lord Byron I like his poetry, his politics and he has some interesting friends.

Michael Foot I admire his intellect, gentleness, and stamina. Great on political history.

Elvis Costello Dark, ironic, bitter lyrics and brilliant melodies. My musical hero.

Mary Wollstonecraft One of the first feminists when they were even more unpopular than they are now.

Inspector Morse My favourite detective; well informed, sarcastic and different.

Charles Dickens Favourite author. Adept social commentator who created lovely characters and discussed all classes.

Bessie Smith Rebel and brilliant singer. What more need I say?

Eleanor Roosevelt Intelligent, thoughtful, humane, and most maligned by the American public.

Jesus I don't need to explain why for him, do I?

Boadicea At last an opportunity to discover something more about the Dark Ages.

At my house, so I don't have to travel – I'm lazy.

location At my house, so I don't have to travel – I'm lazy.

menu Roast potatoes and lager.

music A pre-made tape of all my favourite songs.

toast Let's hope people in the next Millennium can change, stop judging each other on the basis of skin colour and other spurious, pointless, and ultimately unimportant criteria. I hope people will be less cruel to each other and more laid back about claims to mere pieces of land. I also hope people who have hated each other for centuries will be able to forgive.

Boadicea

Germaine Greer

Mary Wollstonecraft

Jesus

29

Bridget Jones
by Helen Fielding

Helen Fielding

Um, 9st 2. Gave up smoking for a total of 27 days last year.

Brad Pitt

Harrison Ford

David Ginola

guests

Jude   Joint best friend.

Sharon   Other joint best friend.

Mr Darcy (or the actor Colin Frith, as he is known) For excellent interpretation of works of Jane Austen.

Prince William   Future King of our land.

Brad Pitt   For contribution to great feminist work, *Thelma and Louise*.

Harrison Ford   For great lifetime contribution to American film industry.

Richard Gere   For tremendous works for Tibetan causes.

David Ginola   For contribution to British football.

Hugh Grant   For great contribution to British film industry.

George Clooney   For tremendous contribution to medical profession.

Nelson Mandela   All admire him tremendously. (N.B. Would probably be best if Mr Mandela just stayed for a drink then went on to something more important, as not sure he would enjoy it later).

location
Sharon's flat – bigger than mine or Jude's. Also downstairs' neighbour hard of hearing.

menu
Starter: M&S smoked salmon pinwheels (36) and Khyber Curry House onion bhajees (24)

Main course: Pizza Express pizzas (various, but nothing with fried egg on, please).

Dessert: Tesco steamed chocolate Belgian puddings with chocolate sauce (12), M&S raspberry pavlovas (4), large if possible.

Après dessert: 4 boxes Milk Tray (very large if possible, please), 4 Chocolate Oranges, 3 large tubes of Cadbury's Mini Eggs.

Drinks: Chardonnay (22 bottles please) Silk Cut (12 packets please). Will give up at midnight.

music   *I Will Survive*.

toast   We do not require any toast thank you as we have enough with the pizzas etc.

George Clooney

George Clooney, for tremendous contribution to medical profession

Kelly Brook

TV presenter and model.

guests Aphrodite Greek goddess of love. To spread love and beauty into the year 2000.
Elizabeth I Will be able to hold her own in the company round the table; sparks are certain to fly between her and Oscar, as their wit competes.
Judy Garland As Dorothy from *The Wizard of Oz* (and Toto). It will be amusing to hear her burst into song at every opportunity.
Hatshepsut The bearded Egyptian queen who became the first female pharoah. She would fascinate us with her tales of ancient Egypt.
Betty Boop [*host*] To be cute and glamorous, and to spill the cartoon gossip.
Oscar Wilde The ultimate dinner guest. I'm sure he would be able to use the evening as material for his next farce.
David Niven For his easy English charm and his dirty Hollywood tales.

James Bond Played by Sean Connery. The sexiest man – not to mention clever, funny, risk-taking and gorgeous. What more could you ask for? (I hope he brings his gadgets!)
Del Boy aka Derek Trotter - *Only Fools and Horses*. What a charmer! Comedy value all round and you stand half a chance of getting some knocked-off gear!
Jesus Just think of the questions you could ask the son of God! Plus his talent of performing miracles could come in handy.
Yoda Star Wars character originally from *The Empire Strikes Back*. The cleverest, oldest 'person' in the universe. Could also teach everyone 'The Force' after dinner.

location A marquee in the Garden of Eden – the most beautiful place I could imagine. Plenty of room for an after-dinner stroll.

menu This is where Jesus comes in handy...we will have five loaves and two fish, and Jesus can turn them into everyone's favourite food. We will also have water and Jesus can turn that into wine and champagne.

music
Karaoke (as follows):
Kelly Brook: *Wake Me Up Before You Go Go* (Wham)
Aphrodite: *Venus* (Bananarama)
Elizabeth I: *Like A Virgin* (Madonna)
Dorothy: *It's Raining Men* (Weather Girls)
Hatshepsut: *Walk Like An Egyptian* (The Bangles)
Betty Boop and Del Boy: *Love Shack* (B52's)
Oscar Wilde: *Common People* (Pulp)
David Niven: *1999* (Prince)
James Bond: *I'm Too Sexy* (Right Said Fred)
Jesus: *I Will Survive* (Gloria Gaynor)
Yoda: *Can You Feel The Force* (The Real Thing)

Betty Boop

David Niven

Oscar Wilde

Elizabeth I

31

Gordon Brown

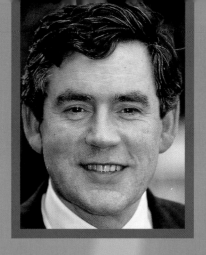

Rt. Hon. Gordon Brown MP.
Chancellor of the Exchequer
and MP for Dunfermline East.

make the eradication of the Third World debt a reality

guests

Nelson Mandela The leader.
Martin Luther King The civil rights leader.
Aung San Suu Kyi The human rights leader.
Mary Slessor The missionary.
Edith Cavell The resistance fighter.
David Lloyd George The prime minister.
J. S. Bach The composer.
William Shakespeare The poet.
Lewis Grassic Gibbon The writer.
Eric Riddell The runner.
Jessye Norman The singer.

location
Washington DC – home of the World Bank.

menu
A wonderful African or South American meal – the food that we would want all the people of these continents to be able to eat.

toast
On the eve of the new Millennium we are gathered here not only in celebration but to begin to make the eradication of the Third World debt a reality. To take action to secure debt relief and poverty relief, action to secure it now so that the world will not carry all of the old injustice into a new Millennium. What inspires all of us here is a vision of a new climate of justice across the world, a new climate of justice that will liberate nations from unsustainable debt, and people from unfulfilled lives, bringing our global economy and our moral universe into harmony for the first time.
Unsustainable debt is a burden imposed from the past on the present which is depriving millions of their chance of a future, and preventing them breaking out of the cycle of poverty, illiteracy and disease. We know that we have obligations beyond our own front door, responsibilities beyond our city walls, duties beyond our national borders. We believe also that we are all called to feed the hungry, shelter the homeless, and help the sick whoever they are and wherever they are. We believe that when there is an injustice anywhere it is a threat to justice everywhere. So let us resolve to stand together and to work together, churches, political leaders, the peoples of Britain and people everywhere in the world. We will become at last a world community, where the strong helping the weak makes us all stronger. Now as never before, we have within our grasp the means to eliminate abject poverty once and for all. This is our call to action.

Nelson Mandela

Martin Luther King

J. S. Bach

Jessye Norman

Julie Burchill

I am a writer and journalist who has published ten books of fiction and non-fiction, including *Married Alive*. I am currently writing sitcoms for BBC1 and Channel 4.

guests

Josef Stalin To get HIS side of the story.
Oliver Cromwell Quite a guy!
Mariella Frostrup The most charming woman in the world. Would made even Cromwell let his hair down.
Kim Philby My hero.
Daniel Raven My boyfriend.
Susan Raven My best friend. Brilliant company.
Marilyn Monroe Just BECAUSE.
Will Self Sexy and brilliant.
Christine Keeler Most beautiful woman in the world.
Sherlock Holmes
Tigger Wouldn't let us take ourselves too seriously.

Stalin

Will Self

seating plan

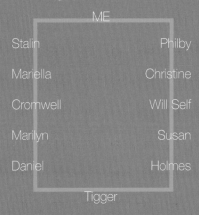

	ME	
Stalin		Philby
Mariella		Christine
Cromwell		Will Self
Marilyn		Susan
Daniel		Holmes
	Tigger	

location Saltdean Lido, Brighton, in July, illuminated by 2000 fairy lights. The most beautiful Art Deco building in England.

menu Steak au poivre, lobster Thermidor, cheese cake, champagne – because I'm working class. An undressed salad and Evian for Cromwell as a tease, because he's meant to be a Puritan.

music Red Army Choir, St Etienne, both live.

toast A toast to the splendid 20th century; didn't we do well!
Then we'd push Marshal Stalin in the pool and all jump in after him.

champagne –
because
I'm
working
class

Christine Keeler

Tigger

Tony Bullimore

Tony Bullimore has been married to his Jamaican wife Lalel for more than 30 years. In the 1960s he became a champion of racial integration in Bristol. A passionate and skilled sailor, he was voted Yachtsman of the Year in 1985. Less than two weeks after his rescue in January 1997, Tony was back on the water.

guests Sir Walter Raleigh He would have a lot to say.
Charles Darwin He would contribute so much to the evening.
Captain Cook A quest man who contributed so much to the past.
Martin Luther King He may teach us a little more for the future.
Neil Armstrong To talk about his walk on the Moon.
Horatio Nelson The Admiral. How would he like to see the 21st century shape up?
Peter Ustinov [*host*] For his wit and humour.
William Shakespeare To tell us a little about his life and dreams.
Nelson Mandela To tell us all about his struggle.

Paul Bagle He fought for his people who were slaves in Jamaica. How would he see life now?
Christopher Columbus He discovered America. How would he see life now?

location 'Fire Fly', Noel Cowards' lovely house in Jamaica. Beautiful hills and stunning views of the sea... the guests would be delighted.

music Ballads of Nina Simone (to start with); Lloyd Webber's *Chariots of Fire* (for the Millennium). Traditional Zulu music towards the end (late into the night).

Gary Bushell

TV critic and broadcaster, read five times a week in *The Sun*. Also sings with The Gonads.

guests

Elvis Presley Elvis is King.
Max Miller The original cheeky chappy. Max's gags and cheerful vulgarity would brighten up any party. Bring the blue book, Maxie.
Kenneth Williams Wit, raconteur, and comic legend. In Ken's company no double-entendre would pass unnoticed.

Diana Dors Forget Dorothy Parker, Dorsy had the best one-liners and she looked a million dollars.
Dolly Parton Funny, sexy, talented...she'd keep Dorsy on her toes.
Rudyard Kipling Would raise the tone of the evening and the sight of Dolly would probably inspire epic ditties.

Horatio Nelson He could enthral us with tales of daring on the high seas.
Del-boy Trotter Well, someone's got to pour the brandy and lucozade cocktails.
Pamela Anderson What has Tommy Lee got that I haven't?
Billy Connolly The funniest man alive.
Merlin If the party got dull, he could conjure something up.

Darcey Bussell

Sean Connery

Mozart the whole way through

guests
Shakespeare
Jane Austen
Sean Connery
Christopher Columbus
Audrey Hepburn
Fred Astaire
Gene Kelly
Dawn French
Jennifer Saunders
Elvis Presley
My husband

location Castle Isla, Scotland.

menu Sushi, saki with champagne, and sparkling mineral water.

music Mozart the whole way through.

toast Hopefully the future will be as exceptional as the past.

Audrey Hepburn

Elvis Presley

Douglas Cameron

Radio and TV presenter since 1961. 25 years with LBC. Received MBE in New Year's Honours, 1999.

The Queen Mother

Hillary Clinton

guests **The Queen Mother** Surely there has been no one with more interesting memories of the 1900's. For me, the icon of the century.

Bob Monkhouse Like me, the Queen Mum loved the variety theatre, especially comedy; that's why I've put Bob next to her. As a dispenser of humour, he's a joy.

Mary Quant Fashion must be represented, and who better than Mary, the populist guru of the sixties?

Andrew Lloyd Webber They often say about music for the theatre, 'They don't write them like that any more', but Lord Lloyd Webber does.

Marjorie Cameron My wife, who, along with me is the least famous person at the table. But she's there because I love her and, because of my job, she's had a lot of experience talking to VIP's.

Professor Winston Robert Winston, Professor of fertility studies, will have influential views on medicine in the new Millennium.

Queen Elizabeth I My one truly historical guest. Her life story's well worth hearing.

David Frost My favourite man from the news and entertainment media.

Hillary Clinton We've heard a lot from Bill, now I'd like to hear Hillary's views on life – past, present and future.

Ian Wooldridge My favourite sports writer. What a way he has with the written word. And he talks a lot of sense too!

Marje Proops Should any of my guests become too tired and emotional, Marje would offer just the right advice – as well as being the life and soul of the party!

Ollie Campbell

Seamus Oliver (Ollie) Campbell. Barbarians, Lions. 22 caps for Ireland, 1976–1984. Two Lions tours: 1980 to South Africa and 1983 to New Zealand.

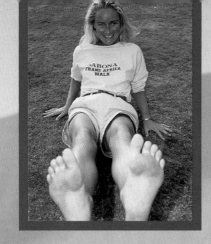

Ffyona Campbell

guests

Two Aboriginal elders
(a male and a female)
For the knowledge, honed
over 40,000 years, of how to
find heaven here on earth,
using nothing but what God
gave them.

Eve and Adam To tell what
really happened to begin
a branch of people who no
longer believe in God's creation.

Billy Connolly To express the
essence of it with humour, hope
and an open mind.

Che Guevara For his belief in
the spirit of human decency and
to give his advice on the way to
spread revolution.

A farm cat (female) One who
crosses between the worlds of
the wild and the tame, who can
tell it from a hunter's perspective
using only what God gave her.

A Soay sheep (female) One
who has remained unchanged
since before Adam and Eve,
who can tell it from the
herbivore's perspective on how
to find heaven on earth.

Jesus To explain how his
teachings are right if they differ
from the laws of God's creation,
Nature.

C.E.O. of Monsanto To listen.

Nelson Mandela One who has
the understanding of how to
love in peace.

location

Around a fire in
the middle of The Great Sandy
Desert, Australia, on a clear,
cool evening with a light warm
breeze from the heat of the
sand as it cools.

menu

Whatever they found,
whatever allowed them to find it,
while out hunting together that
day - and water from a rock
pool, so clear you see the stars
deep inside it.

toast

The Millennium is a
reminder that our spirits have
been invaded and our
capabilities surrendered. The
toast for tomorrow, as for any
other day, is that people will
learn to have faith in their own
abilities once more, to speak
the same language as the
animals and to listen to the
teachings of God's creation so
that everyone finds heaven
here on earth.

I walked around the world.

guests

Karl Mullen Captain of Lions,
New Zealand, 1950.

Robin Thompson Captain of
Lions, South Africa, 1955.

Ronnie Dawson Captain of
Lions, New Zealand, 1959.

Arthur Smith Captain of Lions,
South Africa, 1962.

Mike Campbell–Lamperton
Captain of Lions, New Zealand,
1966.

Tom Kiernan Captain of Lions,
South Africa, 1968.

John Dawes Captain of Lions,
New Zealand, 1971.

Willie John McBride Captain of
Lions, South Africa, 1974.

Phil Bennett Captain of Lions,
New Zealand, 1977.

Bill Beaumont Captain of
Lions, South Africa, 1980.

Ciaran Fitzgerald Captain of
Lions, New Zealand, 1983.

location

Lansdowne Rd,
the oldest international rugby
ground in the world.

music

Soundtrack for the
evening would be the favourite
tour songs as selected by each
of the Captains. What better
way to ring in the new
Millennium than with the World
Cup songs appropriately named
World in Union.

toast

To all the fun and the
memories of the past; to the
diversity of the personalities that
have been the very tapestry of
the game and to the friendships
that have been forged and have
endured throughout the rugby
world over the past century or
so. To the administrators and
players of today. May they show
vision and daring and the
courage of their convictions as
they grapple with the growing
pains of the new professional
rugby order. To the future
generations of the rugby
fraternity. May they continue
to experience the joy and
happiness that have always
been associated with the
game of rugby and above all
else, in an ever-changing and
demanding world, may they
endeavour to retain the true
spirit of the sport.
To absent friends.

Will Carling

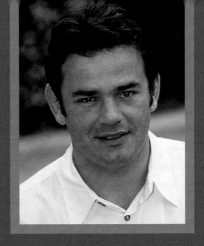

I am quiet and shy and have been very lucky.

guests

Eddy Izzard His humour is brilliant.

Gnasher To eat up any left overs.

Nelson Mandela To listen to his experiences.

Florence Nightingale To keep us all in order, and in case anyone gets ill.

Robin Williams To compete with Eddy Izzard.

C. S. Lewis To tell us stories and say grace.

My mother To do the cooking. She is the best!

Hannibal Lecter To keep everyone on their toes.

Jacqueline Bisset Because I think she is lovely.

Henry Carling Because I want to be with him.

Jacqueline Bisset

Eddy Izzard

Robin Williams

location
A table on the African plains. It is the most amazing experience; the scenery, the noise, the smell.

menu
Very simple: deep fried camembert, very fattening but delicious. Bangers and mash. Red wine. None in particular, but one that would be chosen by C. S. Lewis. I think he would have great taste.

seating plan
It would be a buffet, so people could move around and we could all avoid Hannibal.

music
No music, just listen to the animals.

toast
Thanks for the old Millennium. And a wish for peace, health and happiness for everyone in the new Millennium.

Having acted ever since I can remember, I regard my greatest achievements to be my marriage to Christopher Morahan and my two beautiful, talented daughters.

Anna Carteret

Vesta Tilley... the highest paid Victorian Music Hall artist who dressed in drag to give herself greater freedom of speech

guests Vesta Tilley Married to a conservative MP she was the highest paid Victorian Music Hall artist who dressed in drag to give herself greater freedom of speech.
Elvis Presley One of the sexiest singers in the world, not just his voice, but his whole body.
Germaine Greer For her original mind and provocative sense of humour.
Captain Scott For his courage and sense of adventure.
Maya Angelou For her compelling books and inspiring poems.
Wolfgang Amadeus Mozart For his sublime genius and earthy sense of humour.
Joan of Arc For her bravery and faith against all odds.
Eric Morecambe He would ensure everyone was helpless with laughter.
Claire Tomalin For her ability to bring historical characters to life.
Danny Kaye For his amazing agility and a facility with words.
William Shakespeare For his capacity to depict and understand human nature.

location The foothills of the Himalayas because I love being among mountains.

menu Asparagus shoots. Roast duck, wildrice, red cabbage, apples, onions and mushrooms. Summer Pudding and cream. Champagne, Red wine, Brandy.

music Symphony no. 3 by Henry K Gorecki followed by the complete collection of the Beatles songs (live).

toast Let us learn from the past and broaden our horizons for the good of everyone on earth in the new Millennium.

Maya Angelou

Elvis Presley

Eric Morecambe

Danny Kaye

Justice. May there be more of it in the third Millennium

A runner, competed in the 1952 and 1956 Olympics; held the world 5,000- metre record; was ITN's first newscaster; was an M.P. and a minister in the governments of Harold Macmillan and Edward Heath; chairman of the Civil Aviation Authority.

Christopher Chataway

guests **Admiral John Byng** Guest of Honour. He is a distant relative who, in 1757, was executed by firing squad for cowardice. It was grossly unfair, as subsequent historians have agreed. The purpose of the dinner is to assemble some of the brilliant figures who bravely supported Byng before, during and after his court martial.

Sarah Osborn Byng's sister who campaigned vigorously on his behalf.

Dr Samuel Johnson 18th-century literary lion who wrote a pamphlet urging Byng's innocence.

James Boswell The companion and biographer of Johnson.

Voltaire In whose novel, *Candide*, it is explained that the English like to shoot an admiral from time to time, in order to encourage the others.

Duc de Richelieu The admiral, whose superior Byng wisely refused to attack, wrote later in support of his adversary when he heard of the court martial.

Horace Walpole Author and M.P. – son of the first Prime Minister.

Sir Francis Dashwood M.P. Founder of the notorious Hell-Fire Club. Wild and badly behaved, but spoke out strongly for Byng.

William Pitt (later Lord Chatham) Tory Prime Minister.

Lady Yarmouth (mistress to George II) She helped Pitt into office but too late to save Byng.

Henry Fox Whig M.P. and the only opponent of Byng to be invited. He and Pitt were the outstanding debaters of their generation, so he will add spice to the evening.

location The Royal Naval College, Greenwich, where Byng was imprisoned before his trial.

menu A variety of 18th-century dishes and good clarets. The most demanding guest, undoubtedly, will be Dr. Samuel Johnson, who said, 'He who does not mind his belly will hardly mind anything else.' For him there will be boiled leg of lamb and spinach, which he liked. Also plenty of brandy. 'Claret', said Johnson, 'is the liquor for boys; port for men; but he who aspires to be a hero, must drink brandy.'

seating plan A round table to encourage one inclusive conversation. Fox to sit opposite Pitt and Johnson opposite Voltaire; Byng to sit next to Richelieu, so that the old seadogs can swap yarns when the politicians and writers get on to other subjects; Francis Dashwood not to sit next to either of the women (for their protection): I will sit next to William Pitt since there a mass of things I should like to ask him about 18th-century politics if there are gaps in the conversation; on the other side I shall have Lady Yarmouth so that I may ask her a few indiscreet questions about the King.

toast It was, of course, the Whigs who made a scapegoat out of poor old Byng, so the first toast is: 'Death and damnation to the Whigs. May they roast in hell for at least another Millennium' (or something uncontroversial of that kind).

The second toast is: 'Justice. May there be more of it in the third Millennium.'

Billie Holiday

The Chemical Brothers

Sebastian Coe

location Brixton Academy – our favourite venue.

toast Whilst you're raving, Let's do some. saving

The chemical brothers

guests
General Pattern
Steve Ovett
Sir Roger Bannister
Billie Holiday
Count Basie
Lester Young
Coleman Hawkins
Herb Elliot
Daley Thompson
Vivien Leigh
Kip Keino
Muhammad Ali
Eric Morecambe
Alistair Cook
Woody Allen
Sugar Ray Robinson
Jesse Owens
Ruby Wax
Joanna Lumley
Margaret Thatcher
Dorothy Parker

location At the first ancient Games on the banks of the river Alpheus, by the sandy shore of Elis, in Olympia.

menu We would eat oysters followed by a good pasta dish and drink Rioja red wine.

music We would listen to live jazz played by The Duke Ellington Band.

toast To my family, who have consistently supported me and been my inspiration throughout my life and to my children...for their humour, unpredictability and unconditional love.

Woody Allen

Muhammad Ali

Joan Collins

Actress, author, mother of three. 55 movies, 7 plays, 9 books, 350 hours of television and producer of 3 US mini series.

guests
Scarlett O'Hara Beauty and willfulness and not afraid to speak her mind.
Rhett Butler There could be fireworks with him, which could be exciting.
Noel Coward Every word a gem. The ultimate scintillating wit.
Gertrude Lawrence Charming, amusing, and elegant. Her salty humour was captivating.
John F. Kennedy Charismatic and a great President, not to mention very sexy.
Cleopatra I've always been fascinated by her and I'm sure everyone else would be.

Oscar Wilde A supreme story teller, witty, and a raconteur who will mesmerize the table.
Coco Chanel One of the first liberated women and the most stylish. I love her look.
Charles Lindbergh America's greatest hero. First man to fly the Atlantic, must have a few tips about jet lag.
Marlene Dietrich Arguably the most glamorous woman of the 20th century with a fine line in bitchy put downs.
Marlon Brando at 35. The best looking creature ever. Mean, moody with magnificent sex appeal in spades.

location
Windsor Castle or Versailles.

menu
Champagne – Krug. Pommes Paysanne (baked potato with Beluga caviar) served with orange Stolichnaya vodka. Beef Strogonoff with rice, baby broccoli and purée of spinach, served with Château Lafitte 1961. Pecan pie with caramel sauce and pecan almond ice-cream.

music
Before dinner: 30s & 40s show tunes. During dinner: cool Jazz. After dinner: show tunes around the piano – everyone sings. Followed by: wild Latin American dancing (Samba, Cha-cha, Tango). Then: 70s and 80s Disco music.

toast
May the next one thousand years allow us to slow down the pace of technology a little more. May peace come to the world that has known so much conflict and strife, and may prosperity come to those who have not known it. May mankind use his mind instead of machines, and let us clean up our polluted atmosphere so our children can thrive.

Dietrich... Arguably the most glamorous woman of the 20th century

Terence Conran

Terence Conran is a designer, retailer, restaurateur and entrepreneur. His current businesses include ten Conran shops around the world, restaurants in London, Paris, New York and Stockholm, and the architecture and design group, Conran and Partners. He is also the author of more than twenty books.

guests

Victoria Davis For love.

My mother For inspiration.

Noel Coward For English *bon mots*.

Dorothy Parker For American wit.

Henri Cartier-Bresson To capture the essential moment.

Nelson Mandela For humanity.

Marilyn Monroe Because gentlemen prefer... (even when they're peroxide!)

Leonardo da Vinci For brilliance.

Edoardo Paolazzi For friendship and translation.

Harry Houdini For after-dinner entertainment.

James Dyson To clear up!

location

The Tower of London – it's symbolic of London, is full of history, and has great views of the Thames. (And I could keep an eye on business at The Butlers Wharf restaurants!)

menu

Vintage champagne on arrival Langoustines, freshly baked bread and home made mayonnaise, with a Bâtard-montrachet '92. Roast grouse, jus, bread sauce, game chips and broad beans with Château Petrus. Scottish raspberries and unpasteurised cream with Château d'Yquem Simple but greedy!

seating plan

Oh, I'd encourage people to sit where they choose.

music

Stephane Grappelli, Django Reinhardt and The Jazz Club de France would be very jolly. At midnight I'd have the most fantastic firework display over the Thames, accompanied either by Handel's Firework Music or, perhaps, grunting Keith Jarret and his Koln concert.

toast

To serious pleasure: eat, drink and be merry.

To serious pleasure: eat, drink and be merry

Marilyn Monroe

Henry Cooper

After a highly successful boxing career as British, European and Commonwealth Heavyweight champion, Henry Cooper has become a very popular TV personality and a much sought after speaker. He is a regular on *A Question of Sport* and a keen golfer.

guests My five greatest opponents.
Muhammad Ali
Floyd Patterson
Ingermar Johansen
Jo Hoskin
Alex Miteff

venue Wembley Stadium or Richard Sheperd's Langham's Brasserie.

music Stéphane Grappelli.

menu Steak & Kidney Pudding – to be cooked by Delia Smith

Steak and Kidney Pudding recipe (serves 6)

For the suet crust pastry:
12 oz (350g) self-raising flour
6 oz (175g) shredded beef suet
Salt and freshly milled black pepper
Cold water to mix

For the filling:
1¼ lb (560 g) chuck steak
8 oz (225 g) ox kidney after trimming,
so buy 10 oz (275 g)
2 level tablespoons well-seasoned flour
1 medium onion, sliced
Cold water
1 teaspoon Worcestershire sauce
Salt and freshly milled black pepper

You will also need a 2½-pint, 1.5-litre capacity pudding basin and a steamer.

To make the pastry first sift the flour and salt into a large mixing bowl. Add some freshly milled black pepper, then add the suet and mix it into the flour using the blade of a knife. When it's evenly blended, add a few drops of cold water and start to mix with the knife, using curving movements and turning the mixture around. The aim is to bring it together as a dough, so keep adding drops of water until it begins to get really claggy and sticky.

Now abandon the knife, go in with your hands and bring it all together until you have a nice, smooth elastic dough which leaves the bowl clean. It's worth noting that suet pastry always needs more water than other types, so if it is still a bit dry just go on adding a few drops at a time. After that, take a quarter of the dough for the lid, then roll the rest out fairly thickly. What you need is a round approximately 13 inches (32.5 cm) in diameter. Now line the bowl with the pastry, pressing it well all around. Next chop the steak and kidney into fairly small cubes, toss them in the seasoned flour, then add them to the pastry-lined basin with the slices of onion. Add enough cold water to reach almost the top of the meat and sprinkle in a few drops of Worcestershire sauce and another seasoning of salt and pepper.

Roll out the pastry lid, dampen its edges and put it in position on the pudding. Seal well and cover with a double sheet of foil, pleated in the centre to allow room for expansion while cooking. Now secure it with string, making a little handle so that you can lift it out of the hot steamer. Then place it in a steamer over boiling water. Steam for 5 hours, topping up the boiling water halfway through. You can either serve the pudding by spooning portions straight out of the bowl, or slide a palette knife round the edge and turn the whole thing out on to a serving plate (which is more fun!).

Steak and Kidney Gravy

Although steak and kidney pudding has a lovely juicy filling, it's always nice to have a little extra gravy – and since there's always some meat trimmings over, this is a good way to use them.

Meat trimmings from the steak and kidney
1 teaspoon beef dripping
1 heaped dessertspoon flour
1 onion, halved
A few drops Worcestershire sauce
1 pint (570ml) water
Salt and freshly milled black pepper

Simply place the meat trimmings in a saucepan with half the onion, cover with 1 pint of water, add some seasoning and simmer for approximately 1 hour. Then strain the stock and in the same pan fry the remaining onion, chopped small, in the beef dripping until soft and blackened at the edges. Then stir in the flour, gradually add the stock little by little to make a smooth gravy, adding a spot of gravy browning if it's needed. Taste to check the seasoning and add a few drops of Worcestershire sauce.

from *Delia Smith's Winter Collection* by Delia Smith. Reproduced with the permission of BBC Worldwide limited. Copyright © Delia Smith.

Writer of about 37 books and seven plays.

Jilly Cooper

Only one main course offered to prevent an anxious situation for doubting Thomas

guests

Jesus Because he was the greatest, bravest man who ever lived. And I'd like him to have his friends around him.

Peter

Andrew

James

Philip

John

Bartholomew

Thomas

Matthew

James (the less)

Thaddeus

...without Judas

location HEAVEN, The Embankment, London... where the bad boys go.

menu Drink: still water for Jesus to turn into wine as and when needed.
Starter: olives picked from Mount Olive.
Main: bouillabaisse – made from all the fish in the sea of Galilea caught by Saint Peter. (Only one main course offered to prevent an anxious situation for doubting Thomas.)

seating plan I'd like to sit next to Jesus because there are a million questions I'd like to ask him. Occasionally I would lean across and talk to the disciple he loved best who must have been a cracker.

music Verdi's Requiem. Jesus to walk on water half way through as a bit of cabaret.

toast To be given by Pontius Pilate on the theme of truth. I think there would be room for a short apology.

Coronation Street

by John Stevenson on behalf of Jack and Vera Duckworth

Transcript of a discussion between Jack and Vera Duckworth:

JACK: We can have anybody we want at this do? And we don't have to pay for it? Right, we'll have Samantha Fox, we'll have Madonna, we'll have Joanna Lumley, we'll have Linda Lusardi, and Posh Spice –

VERA: I know what your game is you tripehound! Trust you to want a load of trollopes.

JACK: No, no, fair dos, Posh Spice can bring David Beckham with her, I can give him a few tips, improve his game like. And I tell you what – we'll have Fergie as well!

VERA: What? Duchess of York? Oh no...

JACK: No, Alex Ferguson. You know, Man. United. Because I think I've spotted where he's been going wrong.

VERA: See, this is going to be a family do. Just family. So we'll have the Queen, Philip of course, and our Margaret, and Charlie, and the two lads –

JACK: Vera, for the hundredth flaming time, you and Her Majesty are not related.

VERA: Oh yes. Me and her had the same great grandad. King Edward the Seventh. My Dad told me all about it on his death bed.

JACK: Your Dad was telling porkies.

VERA: No, not on his death bed. He wouldn't.

JACK: He would. He was practising for when he got to the Pearly Gates in case Saint Peter told him to clear off. Your Dad was so twisted he could have hid himself behind a spiral staircase.

VERA: Look, me and the Queen are cousins, she's family far as I'm concerned, so if somebody else is paying this is a good time for her to come for dinner. You can sit on her right hand, and I'll be sat on her left hand.

JACK: If we do that how the hell's she going to eat her dinner?

VERA: I'll get some nice paper doilies from the corner shop and we'll have the menu wrote out in French. I've asked Ken Barlow to do it for me, so this is what we'll be having – poisson, pommes frites and purée de petits pois.

JACK: No, beggar that foreign muck. We'll have fish, chips and mushy peas.

David Beckham

Joanna Lumley

Prince William

Madonna

I'm 27 years old, I've got a beautiful little boy, I've sold about 30 million albums and I write most of the music. I'm very happy – old in my mind but young in my heart.

The Cranberries
Dolores O'Riordan

guests   My grandfather   Because, of all people who have passed away, I miss him most!

John Lennon   A great artist and great spirit – I'm sure he would be fun.

Elvis   For obvious reasons.

Robert de Niro   I'd look at him all night!!

Madonna   Out of curiosity!

Chrissy Hynde   'Cos she is a true rock chick!

Morrisey   To hear him complain.

My husband   For love.

Sean Connery   He is one of the loveliest guys I've met (or seen).

My son, Taylor   To show him off. (He'd be under age though – he is 1½ years old)

My manager   'Cos he can hold his drink, get sloshed and give a good massage whilst drunk – oh yeah, Levi!

location   Probably at my house 'cos I love it. It's in the 'Golden Vale' of Ireland and there are so many cool things there.

menu   Seafood, caviar for the champers, salad, pizza (very thin crust!). Miller beer, Guinness, Opus 1 red wine by the box!!, and a few bottles of Cristal champagne!

music   Classical - Mozart, Strauss, Stravinski...whatever I have.

toast   To love, health and happiness! Simple, but true!

Sean Connery

Robert de Niro

Elvis

47

Determined, loyal, generous, a lover of life, never moody and always reliable.

A quiet, down-to-earth person who enjoys life.

Cricket (South Africa)
Steve Elworthy Jacques Kallis

guests Alison Elworthy My wife and soul mate and Matthew James Elworthy My son – the most precious creature on earth. And the rest of my family.

location Satellite in outer space with each person at a window enjoying an incredible view of earth.

menu Cream of sun-dried tomato soup.
'Saturn' seared sirloin steaks.
'Venus' vegetables with a sprinkling of 'star dust'.
Mars bars.
Moët champagne (ice-cold).

music High by The Lighthouse Family.

toast The past is something we can do nothing about but the future we can change. My Millennium motto will be: 'If your life flashes before you, make sure it's worth watching'.

guests Henry Kallis My dad.
Janine Kallis My sister.
Sandra Bullock For obvious reasons.
Mark Boucher Good mate.
Dave Rundle My agent.
Leon Schuster For humour.
Nicky Thorp Thorp Delta car sponsor.
Norman Woods To give back some of the money taken from him on the golf course.
Mary Pierce Celebrity.
Celine Dion Would need music.

location On top of Table Mountain. It's peaceful, and there's no better place in the world than Cape Town.

menu Seafood, chicken and steak; full array of drinks.

music Any relaxing music balanced with some dance music.

If your life flashes before you, make sure it's worth watching

Sandra Bullock

Cricket (New Zealand)

Chris Cairns

Brad Pitt

guests Michael Jordan • Kelly Brook [*host*] • Bruce Springsteen • Jennifer Aniston • Brad Pitt • Dawn French • Robert de Niro • Joanna Lumley • George Best [*host*] • Jenny McCarthy • Ian Botham

location Turtle Island in Fiji.

menu Italian food; Jack Daniels, Red Bull, wine.

music U2 playing live and unplugged, supported by Neil Diamond.

Roger Twose

guests Claire Forlani • Shalene Grey (my partner) • Michael Jordan • Blair Milnes (friend) • Elizabeth Shue • Robin Williams • Richard Twose (brother) • Karen Twose (sister) • Jesus Christ • Captain Cook • Marco Polo

location Mystic.

menu Seafood chowder; scallops, smoked salmon, crayfish, fillet steak; selection of sorbets; Crown lager, Moët et Chandon champagne, Cloudy Bay Sauvignon Blanc (New Zealand), Te Kairanga Pinot Noir (New Zealand).

Chris Harris

guests Princess Diana • Michael Jordan • Tiger Woods • John Travolta • Heather Locklear • Robin Williams • Dawn French • Jennifer Saunders • Elle McPherson • Bill Clinton • Mr. Ed

location Castaway Island, Fiji.

menu Lobster, king prawns. Appleton's rum, Jack Daniels, Dom Perignon champagne, cocktails.

music Bruce Springsteen, U2, Van Morrison.

Robin Williams

Princess Diana

49

Lara Croft

I'm the heroine of the internationally acclaimed computer game series, *Tomb Raider*, during which negotiate dangerous and complex environments, solve puzzles, fight savage beasts and perform acrobatic stunts on a daily basis: all in the name of retrieving ancient artefacts. Despite being purely fictitious, I'm flattered to be described as 'one of the most influential characters of the twentieth century' and an 'icon for a generation'! I only hope that this inspires others to follow in my footsteps...

guests **Brian Blessed** One of my aspirations is to piggy-back him up Mount Everest. His determination intrigues me, but he doesn't appear to be having much luck by himself.

Indiana Jones Any man who continually risks his arm for a fedora hat warrants an invitation...and a whip goes a long way in my book.

An ancient Pharaoh Or anyone who respected themselves enough to design such harsh tombs to be buried in and hence give me a task in life. Nobody goes to that kind of trouble anymore.

Winston my butler. Although I doubt he'd make it: he's lived in my mansion for a good few decades but he still has trouble finding his way around.

Huckleberry Finn my favourite character for a one-to-one.

My aunty So long as she brings her vicious Corgi – I enjoy small, fast-moving targets.

Will Smith For pure comedy and entertainment value.

Steven Spielberg For his dogged pursuit in bringing extinct and highly interesting species to life.

James Bond So that I could give him a few tips.

Jennifer Aniston Because she's worth it. And I think we need to balance numbers.

location Somewhere remote – with a good tomb nearby. Perhaps ancient Peru. My guests would have an adventure simply finding the place – and would arrive suitably dishevelled so as not to make me look too scruffy for the occasion in my rather battered shorts and leotard. Personally I find evening dress rather unflattering since my gun holsters tend to stick out somewhat.

menu Have to admit that beans on toast is my favourite snack and vastly improved when accompanied by quality champagne. I'd also consider a rather interesting cocktail that was once presented to me by a tribe in the Amazon rainforest – a sort of initiation I think. The drink in question is said to endow the consumer with the 'powers of the light' – I certainly found the peculiar taste and following sensation rather enlightening, although I did end up with a blinding headache... perhaps that's what they meant?

seating plan Provided it's dry, I've always found a blanket under the stars very comfortable so I think I'd organise my guests to bring their own sleeping bags and mosquito nets – one has to consider the comfort of others. As for the actual plan, I suppose I might have to consider a fenced enclosure for guests to protect them from any savage natives and wild animals – a

Steven Spielberg

Jennifer Aniston

Harrison Ford (Indiana Jones)

welcome addition to the evening's entertainment for me, but I think some of my guests would find it all a bit too much.

music
The natural sounds of wild animals and the beat of tribal drums in the distance, a scattering of gunfire...the odd explosion...

toast
Old Millennium: silicone is not the answer, but it got me where I am today and will always be a part of my life.
New Millennium: to adventure and discovery – may we all achieve our goals.

silicone is not the answer, but it got me where I am today

LaraCroft.

Caroline Crumby

I joined Sothebys Restaurant in March 1996 as head chef. The menu, which changes daily, has enjoyed excellent reviews and made the restaurant a hugely popular London lunch spot.

guests Marlon Brando Mr. sex god. Elizabeth Taylor Glamour incarnate – 20th-century Cleopatra. Richard Burton Witty, urbane raconteur. Han Solo Outer space adventurer with lots of good stories to tell! Dorothy Parker Good at the put-down – need a bitch. George Harrison My favourite of the Fab Four. Cleopatra What was she really like? Denise Van Outen Party gal. Elvis Presley Those looks, those hips, that voice... Carrie Fisher Makes me laugh. Jools Holland Mischievious jazz afficionado.

location In outer space – to see the first sunrise of the new Millennium.

menu Homemade roast fennel, artichoke, field mushroom, feta and wild rocket pizza; Nectarine, blackberry, toasted almond and vanilla ice-cream sundae; Champagne cocktails.

seating plan Round table with Elvis at 12 o'clock and clockwise as follows: Denise, George, Dorothy, Richard, Cleopatra, Marlon, Carrie, Han, Elizabeth, Jools.
I would sit Richard Burton and Carrie Fisher next to their screen paramours just to see if there was any real life chemistry; Marlon Brando's famous difficultness could easily be handled by two such strong women as Cleopatra and Carrie; The intellectual element could be provided by Dorothy and Richard, who could spar and talk about Dylan Thomas; Elizabeth Taylor might consider Han Solo a possible future husband and have a laugh with Jools, who, in turn, could talk rock 'n' roll with the 'King' till the cows come home; Denise Van Outen could easily have been a beach babe from Blue Hawaii, so Elvis could feel comfortable with her whilst George might be a fan of The Big Breakfast.

music Elvis Presley karaoke session.

toast When I was a child, knowledge was my heart's desire – I wanted to know anything and everything. The world seemed so exciting and full of possibilities – it still is – here's to the future...

Jools · Denise · Elizabeth · George · Han · Dorothy · Carrie · Richard · Marlon · Cleopatra

Elizabeth Taylor might consider Han Solo a possible future husband

recipes

Roasted Fennel, Artichoke, Field
Mushroom, Feta and Wild Rocket Pizza
(serves 2)

Pizza Dough:
6 oz plain flour
4 fl oz milk
1 tbsp. olive oil
½ sachet easy blend dried yeast

Topping:
1 large fennel bulb
1 medium red onion
2 cloves garlic, peeled
1 tbsp. sprigs fresh thyme
½ tsp. whole fennel seeds
½ can artichoke hearts, drained and halved
2 oz unsalted butter
2 large flat field mushrooms
2 handfuls wild rocket
3 oz plain feta
2 fl oz olive oil

1. First make the dough – mix the flour
and yeast, add the milk and the oil and
knead for 10 minutes to a smooth, soft
and springy dough. Put into a lightly oiled
bowl and cover with a damp cloth. Leave
to rise in a warm place, to double in bulk,
for approximately 2 hours.
2. Meanwhile, slice the fennel, onion and
garlic and mix with fennel seeds, olive oil,
rock salt and ground black pepper. Roast
this slowly at oven 300°F. for approximately
1–1½ hours, until vegetables have softened.

Dot the mushrooms with butter, season and
grill for 5–10 minutes, then cool and slice.
3. When dough is ready, knock it back to
original size and roll into pizzas of whatever
size, shape and thickness wanted. Preheat
oven to its highest setting and heat baking
trays for 10 minutes, then lightly dust them
with flour.
4. Assemble topping on pizza – fennel mix
first, then mushrooms and artichoke. Bake
for approximately 5–10 minutes. Once out
of oven, crumble over feta and scatter over
rocket.

Nectarine, Blackberry, Toasted Almond
and Vanilla Ice-Cream Sundae

2 large, ripe, juicy nectarines
1 punnet fresh blackberries
1 tub good vanilla ice-cream
2 oz lightly toasted flaked almonds
¼ pint double cream and 1 tsp. icing sugar,
lightly whipped

Roughly chop nectarines and build up
layers of fruit and ice-cream. To taste, top
with whipped cream and toasted almonds.
Depending on how sweet a tooth you have,
mix 1 tbsp. caster sugar with the fruit as
this will greatly enhance its flavour.

53

Niamh Cusack

I am a mother and an actor. I have worked in theatre, television and film. I am Irish and will be 40 in 2000.

guests

Maureen Cusack My mother, who died 21 years ago. What would she make of it all?

Finbar Lynch He is the father of my son and I live with him.

Calam Lynch My son – just because no celebration would be complete without him.

Samuel Beckett I love his plays and both his vision and humour would be a treat.

Victoria Wood In one of her personas she would make me laugh and think.

Red Hugh O'Donnell Irish hero who fought for what he belived in.

Christy Moore I think he would be great company and I love his music.

Mikhail Baryshnikov To dance and flirt with.

Sam Sheppard To talk to and flirt with.

Julian of Norwich Great thinker who I've never had time to read. I'd listen to her talk.

Georgia O'Keefe I'd be fascinated to talk to her.

location

Dusk on a summer's evening on Dalkey Island, Co. Dublin (an island about a mile from Dalkey, Co. Dublin where I was born). One of the most beautiful places in summer where we often picknicked as children.

menu

Barbecue of swordfish, tuna, lamb, chicken and Hicks sausages (local pork butchers!); corn on the cob; salad of mixed leaves, avocado, pine nuts, carrots and nuts; home-made coleslaw; potato salad; baked potatoes; Fruit salad (everything exotic); sorbets; bread of every variety; Best white wine; champagne.

music

Irish songs and traditional music – the Bothy Band and Planxty and Christy Moore.

toast

May our spirits toast the next Millennium and may we have achieved peace and wisdom by then. And 'Hurray' for humanity and the throbbingness of living.

Laura Davies

Four time women's Major golf Champion

Michael Jordan

John Lennon by NAYLOR

Christopher Dean

A quiet skater

Audrey Hepburn

guests

Colin Dean My father
Fred Astaire
Audrey Hepburn
John Lennon
Muhammad Ali
Oscar Wilde
Lord Byron
Ayrton Senna
Bob Fosse
Mozart
Cleopatra

menu Pâté de foie gras
Roast chicken with stuffing,
roast potatoes, Yorkshire pudding,
carrots and peas; Tiramisu;
Vintage Lafite-Rothschild.

music Cool Jazz.

toast Happy new year.
With you all here I wouldn't dare
give a speech.

Fred Astaire

guests

Fred Couples • Michael Jordan • Seve Ballesteros • Princess
Diana • Beau Jackson • Kevin Keegan • Alan Shearer •
Michael Owen • Ian Botham • Frankie Dettori • Sean Connery

location Sydney Harbour.

menu Beluga caviar • Fillet steak with potatoes and vegetables
of people's choice • Chocolate mousse • Cheese and biscuits •
Diet coke and Dom Perignon.

music Madonna, Oasis, Spice Girls, Rolling Stones.

toast Good luck to everyone in the new Millennium.

Ian Botham

Princess Diana

Dennis the Menace

Though closing fast on 50 years of age I look remarkably youthful and sport natty black shorts to show off my famous knees. I am the original punk and am proud to be known as 'the world's wildest boy'. Me and my dog Gnasher are stars of one of Britain's favourite comics, *The Beano*.

guests Attilla the Hun A menace from the past.
Genghis Khan A bit of a rascal.
Vlad the Impaler Could be a bit high-spirited.
Darth Vader Cosmic Menace.
Taz, the Tazmanian Devil One of Gnasher's heroes.
A Rangers fan Good for some friendly rivalry.
A Celtic fan Good for some friendly rivalry.
Freddie Kruger My kind of rogue.
Vinnie Jones Enjoys a bit of rough and tumble.
Minnie the Minx My kind of girl.
Layla The lovely Afghan hound down the road. Requested by Gnasher – stop drooling, boy.

location Our house. This would save me and Gnasher a bus fare and, anyway, Dad's keeping us in till May 2003 for being a teensie bit naughty.

menu Jelly, ice-cream, gigantic cream pies, mashed potato, thick lumpy blancmange, squirty tomato sauce, pea soup and chocolate snowballs. In fact, anything messy that can be thrown easily. Let's be honest, the conversation wouldn't amount to much more than grunts and growls, and the table manners would be disgusting, but the food fight would be ....ABSOLUTELY DEVASTATING!

seating plan The Rangers and Celtic fans should sit next to each other and the rest can sit where they like. Who is going to argue with any of that lot? Gnasher has made his knee available for Layla the Afghan hound.

music The music should include Metallica, Iron Maiden, Black Sabbath, The Beastie Boys, and Des O'Connor played at full volume. I don't like my neighbours, you see.

toast May the coming Millennium allow ALL the children in the world to have as much fun as me and Gnasher always have.

Metallica, Iron Maiden, Black Sabbath, The Beastie Boys, and Des O'Connor played at full volume

Desperate Dan

Well, I'm a tad shy about giving my age away but I first appeared in Issue 1 of *The Dandy* way back in 1937. Since then I've been the roughest, toughest, rootin'-tootinest cowpoke in all of comic-land and I don't plan on retirin' just yet.

guests **Hercules** At last! Somebody who will be a little bit of competition for me at arm wrestling.
Conan the Librarian He's not the same since he started reading but I'd invite him for old time's sake.
Sharpe This guy survived a war with the French and then made a TV series about it.
Stone Cold Steve Austin WWF superstar and modern day tough guy. Wrestling him would make a change from grappling with crocs.
John Wayne Him an' me can swap cowboy stories.
William Wallace Like me, a Braveheart hero, but I don't wear emulsion on my face.
Xena, warrior princess My kinda girl – real pretty an' tougher than a grizzly with a sore head.
Tarzan King of the Jungle. Best tell him we dress for dinner round here…or at least put clothes on.

Goliath A real big dude. But is he big enough to eat a whole cow-pie?
Arnold Schwarzenegger Just to let the movie star see us real tough guys up close.
Earl Tupper Not really a tough guy but this feller invented tupperware for a laugh, so he'd be real useful for arranging the eats at the shindig.

location Our front room at home in Cactusville.

menu Easy-peasy. The main course has got to be cow-pie – a full sized one for each of us – no titchy little breakfast-sized ones. Plenty of beans, too, though I have to be careful – last time I had too many beans I started hurricane Betsy. All washed down with my favourite, owl hoot juice, made in a tin bath to a secret recipe, by my old grandpappy.

seating plan These folks can sit where they please – it don't bother me none. As long as they don't sit between me and my food.

music I'm a cowboy at heart so I'll go for some good stomping' country music. If our local band, The Cactusville Mudstompers, are busy, I'd get The Kentucky Headhunters or somebody like that. Just the music for a good ol' down-home ho-down.

toast Well, I ain't the most profound dude in the West, but I always reckon: 'Real tough guys ain't scared to laugh.'

Real tough guys ain't scared to laugh

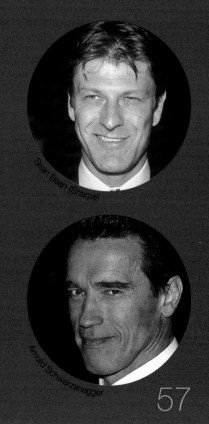
Sean Bean (Sharpe)

Arnold Schwarzenegger

57

Clarissa Dickson Wright

(Two Fat Ladies)

Clarissa (shown left) is 'a cook, TV presenter, entrepreneur, bon viveur and hedonist, with the survival skills of a successful alley-cat'.

guests

Charles II, King of England Wit, lover of good food and wine, great lover – dead sexy and a good dancer.

Oscar Wilde Playwright and poet. Great wit and raconteur.

Fourth Marquis of Bute Great builder, collector and author of English-Moroccan cookery book.

Richard Burton The Arabist and explorer.

Charles II, King of England

location
The Great Hall of Lennoxlove House by Haddingfer, East Lothian, Scotland.

menu
Sevinga caviar with Stolichnaya • Lobster by Mme Prunier with Taittinger Blanc de Blanc • Truffled Dodo cooked by Escoffier with Pernand-vergelesses • Wing rib of beef on the bone cooked by me with Gevrey-chambertin • Ambrosia cooked by Carême

the first tune of the new Millennium:
Ra Ra Rasputin by Boney M

Raconteur, traveller, storyteller and expert on rare sexual practices.

Robert Burns Raconteur, romantic poet, sex-pot and a good dancer.

Thomas Telford Builder. Any man who can hold together an aqueduct with melted sugar has to be good value.

Catherine of Bragenza Wife of Charles II. Intelligent, witty and forthright. Good dancer.

St Teresa of Avila Saint and wit. Intelligent, witty and forthright.

Eleanor of Acquitaine Queen of England and France. Started the court of romantic love and built hostels for battered wives.

Princess Pauline Borghese Sister of Napoleon Bonaparte. Witty, hedonistic and beautiful.

Bess of Hardwick Jailer of Mary Queen of Scots and powerful Tudor female. Great builder.

with Château d'Yquem • Soft herring roes on toast • Stilton with Fronsac.

music
Throughout the meal we would have the music of the harpist David Watkin. At midnight the pipes and drums of the Scots Guards would leads us in *Auld Lang Syne*, and the first tune of the new Millennium – *Ra Ra Rasputin* by Boney M.

toast
That every person may have enough to eat, a roof over their heads, and to paraphrase Henry IV of France, 'chicken in their pot once a week'… and let it be free range.

Oscar Wilde

St Teresa of Avila

Lee Dixon

Lee Dixon has played professional football from a very early age, signing for Arsenal in 1988. He has collected 21 caps for England. He enjoys nothing better than a round of golf with his mates.

guests

Arnold Palmer I have always had a great love of golf and I admire him greatly.

Muhammad Ali He is a great sportsman and someone who has campaigned hard for equal rights amongst black people. He always takes time out for his fans, even now when he is sadly very ill.

My wife I am very much a family man and the Millennium just would not be the same if she were not there to celebrate it with me.

Madonna She is very talented. I would love to see if she really is such an extrovert.

Stephen King I read a lot of his books and would like to see whether he is really that macabre.

Adolf Hitler Just to see whether the moustache was for real!!

Jo Brand [*host*] Great sense of humour and I think she would keep the party going through the night.

Ayrton Senna I have a great passion for Grand Prix racing and used to really enjoy watching him race.

Pele One of the most prolific players of our time.

Gary Dixon I would have to have my brother there – he would kill me if I had such an amazing dinner party and did not invite him.

Audrey Hepburn Very beautiful actress. I would love to know if she was as serene off-screen as she was on.

location
At a château in France.

music
'Bat out of Hell' is my all-time favourite track – at least it would keep my guests awake.

menu
As a starter, any sort of seafood would be great, then roast chicken, and fresh fruit to finish. Not very exciting, but my absolute favourite.

Neil Dishington

FANTASY FEAST 2000

HOST YOUR OWN MILLENIUM PARTY

DISH

'I THINK HE'S HAD ENOUGH PUNCH'

Arthur Dodd

My name is Arthur Dodd. I am 79 years old. From a carefree childhood and a youth stolen by the principles of a war which witnessed 'Satan' at his best, I returned home to find a marriage and children. My greatest achievements are my unshakeable faith, my family and my forgiveness.

guests

Hearts of Stone

Adolf Hitler

Heinrich Himmler

Dr Josef Mengele

Gertrud Klink

Rudolf Hess

Hearts of Gold

Primo Levi

Maria Koska

Anne Frank

Leon Greenman

Medical officer Capt Spencer

Corporal Purdy

location
The gas chamber at Auschwitz. The prisoners of war would like the men responsible for their plight to see the surroundings they endured...the luxury and comfort.

menu
Hearts of Stone: Buna potato soup and water.
Hearts of Gold: caviar and champagne.

seating plan
5 Hearts of Stone facing 5 Hearts of Gold.

music
Beethoven's *The Egmont Overture* – a favourite of Dr Mengele at the selection each morning. This music would, no doubt, make the Germans feel at home.

toast
As we leave one Millennium and welcome the next, let us hope man can cease inflicting unspeakable inhumanities, the like of which I witnessed at Auschwitz, upon his fellow man. I was incredibly lucky to survive and live the wonderful experience of bringing up a family. I did, however, pay the price; that price was indeed a high one, affecting the very quality of my life. Let us toast the hope that, before his weapons of destruction become such that the very planet is threatened, man can learn to live in a harmonious place and in peace with all his brothers in the new and, as yet, untarnished Millennium.

Arthur Dodd is the subject of the book 'Spectator in Hell' by Colin Rushton, published by Pharoah Press.

My greatest achievements are my unshakeable faith, my family and my forgiveness

Adolf Hitler

Anne Frank

Heinrich Himmler

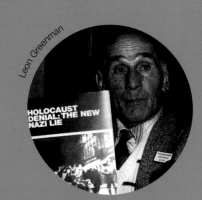

Leon Greenman

An environmentalist since 1956. Co-founder of SustainAbility (1987). Author or co-author of 15 books, including *The Green Consumer Guide* (1988), *Cannibals With Forks* (1997) and *The New Foods Guide* (1999). Chairman of SustainAbility and of The Environment Foundation.

John Elkington

location It is 1 January 2000. Twelve of us have gathered on the Moon, to watch Earthrise. We sit on a gigantic Persian carpet, with a picnic hamper in front of each guest. The silence is ethereal, the spectacle of the Blue Planet literally out of this world.

guests Eve mother to us all, they say. I would like her to see what has become of her line – and to explain that diving into the fruit platter and allowing us all access to Knowledge was a great move.

Salah Al Din better known in the west as Saladin. The military genius who was the Christian crusaders' most effective – and chivalrous – foe.

St Francis of Assisi A man with a magnetic personality, advocating fraternal charity and total poverty for his followers. He was a lover of life and nature, which he saw as a mirror of God. I expect him to take particular pleasure in observing distant Earth.

Sir Walter Raleigh The English adventurer and favourite of Queen Elizabeth I. Among other things, he was a soldier, sailor, captain of the Queen's guard, explorer and relatively humane coloniser of the New World.

Tatanka Iyotake, better known as Sitting Bull. Was the Teton Dakota Indian chief under whom the Sioux tribes finally united in their struggle for survival on the Great Plains. A man of great courage and wisdom his visions led to the defeat of the hot-headed General Custer at the Little Bighorn. Sitting Bull was a loving father of his people, a singer of songs, and a profoundly spiritual man.

Sir Winston Churchill The man who led Britain – and the free world – from near defeat to victory in World War II. I loved the Toad-like bombast and bravado of his early years, but have been moved to tears when reading some of his speeches. His use of English defies description.

Amelia Earhart Crossed the gender divide in her Lockheed Electra. The first woman to fly the Atlantic alone.

Rachel Carson Was a prophet in very much the same way that Sitting Bull was. Happily, her warnings in books like The Sea Around Us and Silent Spring, were soon heeded – indeed, her work catalysed the birth of the environmental movement. Something of an ecological saint, her writing was pure poetry.

Katherine Hepburn Has a special place in my affections. I have always loved cantankerous women. A spirited actress, with more than a touch of Yankee eccentricity.

Joyce Grenfell Whose comic monologues might need to be explained to the likes of Eve, Salah Al Din and Tatanka. Her idea of happiness was 'the sublime moment when you get out of your corsets at night'.

Toad of Toad Hall (modern immortal of Wind in the Willows fame), representing all amphibians and the web of life, celebrating the technology that got us to the Moon ('Toot, Toot!') and savouring the waters as no human could.

seating plan Given the guest list, it is hardly surprising that we decide that rules are to be broken.

Once the group hologram has been created for the purposes of Fantasy Feast 2000, we spring a pleasant surprise: one of the hampers turns out to be a version of Dr Who's Tardis – disgorging the families of each of our guests, plus (to remind us of what it was like) each guest at the age of seven.

toast Before we propose the toast, we watch beamed-in contributions from: several of the astronauts and cosmonauts, (including Yuri Gagarin, the first man to travel in space, in 1961), who were the first to see Earth from the outside.

Professor James Lovelock, on his Gaia theory, explaining how the world works together as if it were a single living entity. And from Stewart Brand and his colleagues at the Foundation of the Long Now, where they are planning to build a clock that will tell time for the next 10,000 years – and remind us, in the process, of the need to think long term. Then the three-fold toast is proposed:

'To Gaia...............
......to those who push the envelope...
and to our common future'...........

Bill Emmott

Bill Emmott, 43, is editor of *The Economist*.

guests

Marilyn Monroe To sing *Happy Birthday* to the Millennium.

Adam Smith To lead the main discussion on freedom.

Karl Marx To eat humble pie at his wrong forecasts of class war and immiserisation.

Thomas Malthus To eat even humbler pie at his wrong forecasts of population doom and starvation.

Friedrich Hayek To gloat at Karl Marx.

Martin Luther-King To broaden the discussion on freedom.

Peter Sellers To impersonate the other guests, and many we couldn't invite.

Frederick Chopin To play the piano.

Jane Austen To offer biting social commentary, and to suggest marriage partners for all the guests.

Sir Isaiah Berlin To explain why Marx was wrong.

Joseph Conrad To tell stories, and relate the whole event to the human condition.

location An enlarged space shuttle, so we could marvel at the earth and at scientific progress.

menu Simply the best organic produce and wine, to make Malthus feel even more guilty at his forecasts of world starvation.

seating plan They would be free to choose their places at a round (because equal) table.

music Chopin's piano compositions (played by Chopin).

toast To freedom, in all its forms (after *Happy Birthday*, sung by Marilyn Monroe).

Marilyn Monroe to sing Happy Birthday to the Millennium

Derrick Evans
Mr Motivator

Mr Motivator runs, amongst other things, fitness classes on GMTV: 'I would like to be remembered as the person who put a smile on everyone's face.'

guests Dr Martin Luther-King A man who whose dream is still alive today. His words live on for all to hear.

Nelson Mandela It is unbelievable that someone can be incarcerated for the length of time he was and, after losing his freedom and then regaining it, feel no ill towards his captors. I would want to know how? And why not?

Sammy Davis Jnr He came through all the prejudices and racism of 50s and 60s and proved that through hard work and determination, no one can stand in the way of our destiny.

Tommy Cooper He would provide the light relief. When the whole table became too serious on any particular topic, he would take the most complicated situation and make everyone laugh at it.

Princess Diana Through her big eyes and subtle smile, she would remind all of us that real lasting beauty comes from within.

Rachel Ward I have always lusted after this woman since I saw her in *The Thorn Birds*.

Marilyn Monroe There is so much I would love to know about her, and to hear it directly from her mouth, listening to her voice, watching her body, would be like ice cream on a very hot day.

Jennifer Lopez There is something about this Latin beauty... she has everything... great voice, every bit a woman, a close second to my wife.

Michael Jackson His life and very existence has touched so many lives. He is unique and to have him as a dinner guest is a must.

Paul Simon A childhood hero whose songs took me through so many of my good times and supported me through the bad. What were the inspirations for so many of his songs, especially *Bridge Over Troubled Water*?

Sandra Evans I would need her help in controlling my excitement at lusting after so many beautiful women, and for wiping the tears from my eyes when the time came for them to go home.

location My house in Jamaica.

menu King Prawns done in butter and garlic • Lamb chops grilled and lightly seasoned • Salmon grilled with a dash of butter • Salt fish fritters • Plantains, rice & peas, spinach, cabbage • Apple crumble and ice cream.
Papaya juice, fresh orange juice, mango juice...all with a hint of rum.

Roy
Nixon

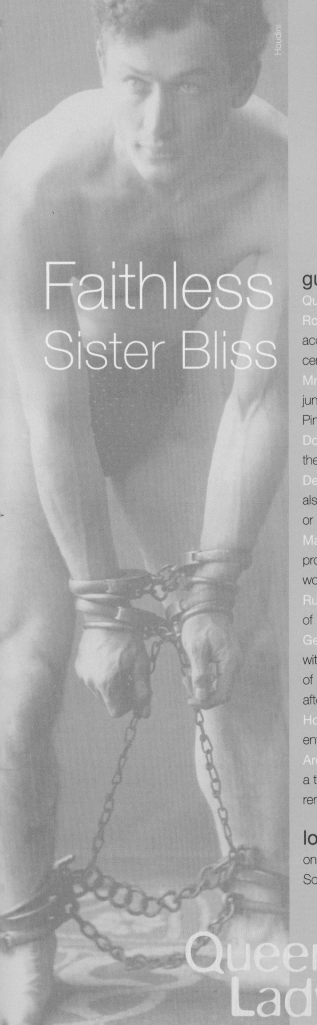

Houdini

I am a DJ, musician and producer whose most successful project to date is the band Faithless. We have sold over four million records worldwide. I think our music is truly millennial because it has global appeal; it has an emotional impact which connects us with those who, superficially, seem very different from ourselves.

Faithless
Sister Bliss

guests

Queen Elizabeth I Lady with an attitude.
Ron Hardy DJ and innovator who accidentally changed the face of 20th-century culture by inventing Acid House.
Mr Brown Inspirational teacher I had at junior school who let us paint pictures to Pink Floyd.
Doris Stokes To keep us in touch with the spirit world.
Deepak Chopra New age guru who is also a 'proper' doctor, in case of medical or spiritual emergency.
Madonna Friend of Deepak's and also probably the most famous woman in the world today.
Rullo My partner in crime and co-founder of Faithless.
George Orwell Writer and humanist with great vision and passion; my level of awareness of the state of society rose after reading his novels.
Houdini Essential for the evening's entertainment.
Aretha Franklin Could teach Madonna a thing or two, and lead us all in a drunken rendition of Auld Lang Syne.

location

The ideal spot would be on top of Table Mountain, Cape Town, South Africa, where you can see the most incredible view and the curvature of the earth. It would also be summer.

menu

A selection of the Cape's finest fresh fish, exotic vegetables and fruits with preferably a top French chef (Michelin-approved) to put it all together. This would be washed down with a combination of the finest champagne, freshly squeezed juices and smoothies, with a bucket of tequila and absinthe to get everyone going for the party after. Dessert would involve meringues, bread pudding and anything creamy.

music

For the beginning of the evening a selection of mellow music, such as Nightmares on Wax *Smoker's paradise*, Massive Attack, or Blue Lines, moving on to more emotional territory, Faithless, *Sunday 8pm*, and finishing off with the best dance classics of the decade.

toast

I propose a toast to friendships which have endured. To the power of music which transcends all boundaries and gives meaning to my life. A toast to everyone who is trying to raise their compassion for each other and their environment. A toast to the end of racial hatred and a solution to poverty. Ultimately a toast to hope.

Queen Elizabeth I...
Lady with an attitude

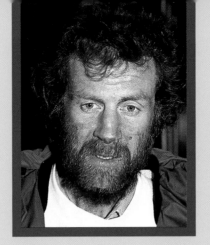

Ranulph Fiennes

Sir Ranulph is a travel writer and expedition leader. Led the first circumnavigation of Earth. First to reach both Poles. First to cross the Antarctic continent unsupported. Discovered lost city of Ubar in Arabia. Fourteen books, two films. £5 million pounds raised for charity.

J. R. R. Tolkien

James Cook

Mahommed

Ptolemy

guests

God He's responsible for it all. Past and Future. He may hear something at the dinner and do something about it.

Jesus God's seat will appear empty. Jesus is the human face of the creator (to many present at the dinner).

St Francis of Assisi He represents at the dinner all the other living things. He'll get on well with Jesus and Tolkien.

J. R. R. Tolkien We need imagination to sort out our problems. Tolkien's imagination is supreme.

Sultan Qaboos of Oman In his own realm he reigns supreme. He has done great things for his people. The ideal living ruler.

Mahommed To achieve a peaceful world, the Muslims must be involved.

Mother Theresa A figure of great hope to children and the sick everywhere. Selflessness personified.

Winston Churchill Saved us from the worst ethnic cleansers known. My personal hero.

Captain Cook The greatest explorer of the Millennium. Opened up the world for trade and understanding.

Ptolemy A great talker. First map of the world. Would map the future with clarity of mind.

Gandhi Violence is our curse, Gandhi its enemy.

location

Stonehenge and a marquee in the V. K. colours. The place has atmosphere and is a national asset. It is internationally known.

toast

Read Voltaire's *Candide* for a quick glimpse of our world a little earlier this Millennium. You will see how greatly things have improved for many millions of us. Many religions, rulers, religious leaders and opinion formers have become so much more tolerant. Cruelty and violence, though still a curse, are not as prevalent as they were. The agony of sickness has been reduced for millions. Television and radio educate. Science makes us aware of the need for conservation. We invented the nuclear bomb, yet have not gone over the brink with it. Despite our oft apparent madness, we've survived so many horrors. NATO and the UN are early models for a supreme body that will keep world peace everywhere. I think God at this point will join the toast for our future, with a gentle smile of hope.

Despite our oft apparent madness, we've survived so many horrors

Keith
Floyd

I love giving parties,
I don't like attending them.

Sherlock Holmes & Dr. Watson

Jilly Cooper

Bob Dylan

guests William Brown from Just William. Boyhood hero... I still read the books to this day...they're funny, you know. If you haven't, then you should try it again; you'd still laugh. **Jeeves** Bertie's butler. **Dr. Hastings** Hercules' sidekick. **Dr. Watson** Sherlock Holmes' sidekick. You see, the sidekicks are more interesting because they know all the stories to tell. **Mervyn Peak** A mystical writer to me, amazing and very profound. Writing based on his experiences as a soldier uncovering the concentration camps. A quiet and sinister sort of person who wrote gloomy but powerful stories. **Evelyn Waugh** He should be a good chatterbox. **J.P.Donleavy** All his books are about excessive eating, drinking and shagging – all the good things in life! **Edith Piaf** **Lauren Bacall** (at about 25 years of age) Still watch those black and white Bogart movies. **Jilly Cooper** [*host*] A friend of mine. **Bob Dylan** Never met him, but wrote a birthday thing for him in The Mail for when he was fifty. Just a great fan.

location I'd like to hire one of the monasteries in Metiora in Greece. They are built entirely on the top of precipitous outcrops of rock...sheer-sided and so dramatic. It's unreal how they could have built them – you can't imagine.

seating plan Everyone free – no-one would need name tags because everyone would know who they were.

music Get Bob and Edith to perform and sing for their supper... after they've had it, of course. I think they could do a duet!

toast Let's keep on keeping on.

menu Classic and terribly simple... Masses of Beluga caviar and iced vodka with blinis,and sour cream, chopped, hard-boiled eggs, finely chopped chives and wedges of lemon; Half of simply grilled crayfish – fresh lobster thing – with delicate hollandaise sauce; Miniature roast leg of milk-fed Spanish lamb – Spanish lamb is probably the best in the world...and the very young lamb is the most esteemed. Served very simply with New Jersey potatoes, fresh broad beans, an onion sauce and a very light gravy; Then the most wonderful raspberries and Cornish clotted cream; Then a cheeseboard that will contain great slabs of Roquefort and something called Exploritature (or whatever the French is for explorer...) and a selection of Provencal goats' cheeses. Wines etc... With the lobster – Le Montrachet. With the lamb – Corton. With the raspberries – Château d'Yquem. With the cheese – the most expensive port possible: Quinta do Novale Nacional 1934. Then a very rare Cognac, Hine, from 1943 – the year of my birthday. Then we shall have espresso coffee. And then a large taxi.

Keith Floyd's next television series, *Floyd Around the Med*, will be transmitted on Channel 5 in February, March and April 2000, and will be accompanied by a book published by Harper Collins.

Celebrity DJ, regular at Ministry of Sound: 'I'm a fairly obsessive person when I get into something. I'm very happy at the moment actually, everything seems very cool.'

Seb Fontaine

Steve McQueen

John Lennon

J. R. R. Tolkien

guests Sugs Childhood hero.
John Lennon Childhood hero and greatest song writer.
Chopper Harris Chelsea player – was on the 70s cupwinning side. He was pretty mean at the back.
Ainsley Harriot A guest but someone's got to do the cooking. He cooks a mean BBQ.
Brigitte Bardot Sauciest of all time.
Steve McQueen He's pretty cool. I could get drunk and talk about cars.
Bruce Lee An amazing person all round. He has an amazing control over his body.
James Coburn He's pretty cool. He was actually a student of Bruce Lee, as was Steve McQueen. (Bruce Lee said that if he could make Steve McQueen and James Coburn as one fighter that person would beat him!)
Sean Connery I think every child dreams to be James Bond at one point.
George Lucas For putting on one of the greatest stories ever told.
J. R. R. Tolkien For putting into print one of the greatest stories ever told.

location I'd have it at my house actually – I've got a new conservatory and I'd better get some use out of it.

menu I've got a Vodka collection from all around the world. You could drink as much as you liked as long as no-one finished the bottle. I've got about fifty different ones – like this dirty old brown Vodka from Russia that is something like ninety years old. I do a lot of travelling so can always bring back different Vodkas.
I think BBQ's are quite fun – I like hot and spicy food – we'd get Ainsley to help out.

music When I'm at home I don't really listen to dance music all that much. (Sugs was my childhood hero – it was always an ambition to be in Madness when I left school!!) I've got a bit of everything – I'd dig out the collection and see what I could find.

toast There is such interesting people going to be there that I'd rather listen to them.

Emma Forbes

TV Presenter. Used to co-host the Saturday morning *Live and Kicking* show on BBC. Also *Talking Telephone Numbers* and more recently *Esther*.

guests

Richard Gere Important to have a major heart throb to entertain the guests.

Billy Connolly To keep everyone laughing. He would provide the outrageous humour for the evening.

Graham Clempson My husband. Graham is a brilliant host and I couldn't bear not being with him at New Year.

Jerry Springer As I am sure everyone, like myself, wants the inside gossip on his show! He'd keep the conversation going.

Jerry Seinfeld To do a 20 minute stand-up after coffee.

Kim Basinger Purely to thrill my husband as a New Year's gift.

Armistead Maupin One of my favourite writers. I adored his books 'Babycakes' and 'Tales of the City'.

Bill Clinton Wouldn't everyone like to chat and question him over dinner?

Martha Stewart I'm afraid I'd ask her to 'style' the event. I'd like it to replicate one of her books.

Frank Sinatra We'd be playing his music anyway and it would be great to have a little bit live.

Lily, my daughter At 2 and a bit, you can always rely on her for making sure there isn't a lull in the conversation. She doesn't stop talking.

location
St. Barts, in the French West Indies, on a beach lit with flaming torches and the waves lapping.

menu
Exotic fruit cocktails – alcoholic and non alcoholic.

Food would be the most wonderful beach barbeque. Delicious fresh fish, grilled vegetables, salads. Have to have French fries.

Pudding would be a selection of the most calorific chocolate puddings, cakes etc. money could buy.

music
Frank Sinatra's greatest hits. A true classic; it would be the perfect sound.

Jerry Seinfeld

Jerry Springer

Billy Connolly

Kim Basinger

68

Bella Freud

Bella Freud is one of Britain's leading fashion designers. She started her own label in 1990 after studying fashion and tailoring in Rome.

guests

Mae West Class A wit. Glamourous and sexy.

Leonard Cohen The darkest man, with the most irony and charm. Also terribly sexy.

Saul Bellow Lover of women and a genius.

Esther Freud (my sister) Very good company. Completely wonderful.

Christian Leuboutin Funniest, wittiest, sincere and naughty.

Claudine (fictional character from Colette's 'Claudine' novels) The most capricious and feminine girl ever.

Luis Buñuel The most eccentric and interesting point of view. The best of the surrealists.

Georgiana, Duchess of Devonshire Beautiful, heavenly, very funny and kind. Very wild ways. Loved by all.

James Fox (my boyfriend) Top writer. Nicest, most handsome, interesting, funny and compassionate man.

Lucian Freud (my dad) The most amazing memory for the most interesting, hilarious and fascinating recollections on any subject.

John Malkovich Fascinating, funny, scary and wonderful. Very good company and quite unpredictable. Also kind.

location

Sir John Soane's house in Lincolns Inn Fields. In the library with the red stained-glass windows. The most elegant, cosy house, original and beautiful; an inspiring place to be.

menu

Native Irish oysters, caviar and buckwheat blinis, roasted woodcock, cabbage and chestnuts. Potatoes mashed with olive oil, risotto with white truffles, raspberries and cream, candied orange dipped in chocolate. Krug Champagne (old), Château Lafite '61, Lafite 'Fine' with ice, mineral water. Coca Cola.

music

Leonard Cohen: *I'm Your Man*. Fugees and Wyclef Jean: *Guantamera*. Chuck Berry: *San Francisco Blues*. Any old thing. Or new.

toast

Here's to the present.

seating plan

```
        John M.   Georgiana

Luis                  Christian

Bella                       Mae

Leonard                  Lucian

Esther                     Saul

        Claudine   James
```

Here's to the present

Mae West

Colette

Leonard Cohen

John Malkovich

69

Dave Gaskill

Engineer turned cartoonist – worked on leading South African, Australian, New Zealand and British newspapers.

guests

Ronald Searle He would produce such wonderful cartoons of the feast.

Henry VIII He would show us all how to devour such a feast with gusto.

Rab C. Nesbitt For his sartorial elegance and Govan wit – could double as a bouncer.

Marilyn Monroe For that necessary touch of glamour.

Kenneth Williams A very funny and witty man.

Judy Dench Because she seems a thoroughly warm and elegant lady.

Rory Bremner He'd bring his own guests – Blair, Major, Cook – and we could jeer.

Victoria Wood For a bit of northern culture and fun.

Ray Charles He can sing and play a bit.

Tommy Cooper He could pull the table-cloth from under King Henry.

Eric and Ern For the cabaret (Ern doesn't get to eat, that's all)

location Anywhere but London.

menu Good German beer and bratwurst Fish 'n' chips and mushy peas.

music Jazz, Country and Western, Classical.

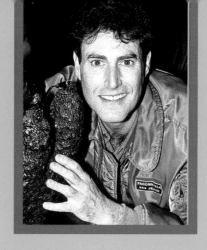

Uri Geller

Uri Geller has been a controversial master of paranormal for more than thirty years. He has been working with people like the Spice Girls and the England football team Coach. One of his bent spoon will fetch thousands of pounds at auctions.

guests

Albert Einstein

Sigmund Freud

Carl Jung

Captain Edgar Mitchell

D.D. Home

Sir William Crookes

Nina Kulagina

Mahomet

Jesus

Moses

Buddha

location Stonehenge. I would obtain permission from the Government to hold the dinner there, and with such an impressive guest list I don't think I would encounter any problems.

menu The food would all be vegetarian, the wines would all be organic and the mineral water would be bottled form the source of the River Jordan – the sweetest water on earth.

music I would play the natural sounds of the jungle, waves breaking upon rocks, and the roar of the waterfalls.

toast I would like to toast all sick people around the world, to those suffering and those in need, and I would wish God's loving and healing touch upon them.

Albert Einstein

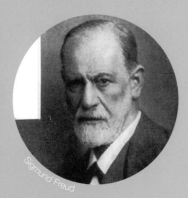

Sigmund Freud

Carl Jung

Buddha

Gene
Martin Rossiter

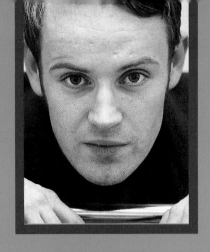

Martin, singer in Gene. I hope dearly that I've made a few people smile.

Dorothy Parker

Mozart

Jaqueline Du Pre

Madonna

guests

Nye Bevan For bluster.
Paul Robeson For me.
Spike Milligan For laughs.
Dorothy Parker For wit.
Olga Korbet For power.
John Toshack For his head.
Mozart For the beer.
Paul Monette For humility.
Jenny Lee For Nye.
Madonna For disco.
Jacqueline Du Pre For beauty.

location Centre circle, Ninian Park, Spiritual Home.

menu I would like to prepare my guests a TV chef each, on a spit, medium rare. Perhaps Ainsley Harriot for Olga Korbet, Anthony Worrell Thompson for Toshack etc. A side dish of corn on the cob, green beans and chips, washed down with Stella.

seating plan Seated on one side of a long table from left to right as follows: Toshack, Spike, Robeson, Madonna, Mozart, me, Monette, Olga, Jennie, Nye, Dot Parker, Jacqueline Du Pre with Ainsley Harriot as decorative table piece (apple in mouth).

music I think they might be able to knock something up between them.

toast An end to fascism.

I would like to prepare my guests a TV chef each, on a spit, medium rare.

Born and raised in Ireland, Grey Gowrie started his career as an academic in American literature. He was a member of Edward Heath's and Margaret Thatcher's administrations and left government service as a Cabinet minister in 1985. He has been Minister for the Arts, Chairman of Sotheby's in Europe and Chairman of the Arts Council of England.

Lord Gowrie

guests Her Majesty Queen Elizabeth the Queen Mother Because she is the life and soul of any party she attends and because she loves the arts.

The Rev. Sidney Smith The greatest Whig wit of his generation, he was exiled for 20 years by the Tories to a poor parish in Yorkshire where he nurtured and entertained his flock as brilliantly as he had London society.

Nancy Lancaster Because she lent me a cottage in her beautiful garden when I was a student, and was a great English hostess who never ceased to be Virginian.

The Duc de Saint Simon He was the incorrupt, maritally faithful Sir Humphrey of the long Regency of the fascinating Philippe d'Orleans, and because his description of life at Versailles makes him the greatest diarist in history.

Kate Croy Because she is the heroine and villain of my favourite novel, *The Wings of the Dove*, by my favourite novelist, Henry James, and because it is clear that James loved her even as she was punished so dreadfully.

Verdi Because although his contemporary, Wagner, is my favourite of the two, he was,

from all accounts, an infinitely kinder and nicer man, as well as a genius.

W. H. Auden Because something by Auden is always in my bag or briefcase, or by my side.

Germaine Greer Because she is the most intelligent conversationalist I have met.

Chardin Because this low key, sensible man was an immortal painter.

Patricia Highsmith Because her novels understand men as well as Henry James understood women.

I have chosen these people because it is my instinct that they would all get on well.

location The Amalienburg Shooting Lodge at the Nymphenburg Palace in Munich, because it is the most beautiful secular interior of the High Baroque, because it is ravishing by candlelight, because Kefer of Munich would do the catering under the supervision of Shaun Hill of Ludow, and because I could bring my Cocker Spaniel, Holly, to try out the Delft-tiled kennels.

menu Built round the small Domaine Romanée-conti vineyard in Burgundy and a great sweet wine of the Moselle.

On arrival Choux pastry cheese puffs and Bollinger 1988.

First course Seared fish foie gras with peeled and seeded Muscat grapes and Sauternes reduction; 1990 Hugel Gewurtztraminer from Alsace.

Fish course Fillet of sea bass steamed in

lettuce leaf wrapping, beurre blanc sauce; Le Montrachet DRC 1979.

Main course Breasts of Irish woodcock, mashed entrails crouton and jus of the pressed carcasses with plain watercress garnish; La Tache 1985.

Salad course Endives with white truffle shavings.

Cheese course Selection of mild ripe cheeses, including Vacherin and Saint Marcellin. Lots more DRC wine, including Romanée-conti 1985.

Dessert Mango sorbet with fresh mango. Maximin Grünhaus Trockenbeerenauslese 1959.

music After the woodcock, W. A. and Constanza Mozart would arrive, join in the festivities and get us all singing. Lonely in Brooklyn in the 1830s, da Ponte would be flown over for a reunion.

toast Your majesty, M. le Duc, Ladies and Gentlemen, thank you all not just for coming to dine tonight but for the pleasure you have given me most of my life, and, less selfishly, for the civilised standards so many of you have set for mankind. I drink to you all, even those, like Kate and Patricia, with such knowledge of the dark places of the heart. I believe that our toast together should be for the Thirteenth at our Feast, who is always with us and whose second Millennium this is. It matters less whether we believe in Him than He in us. May one who understood that feasting and fasting, and pain and pleasure are the fabric of mankind, and whose first miracle rescued a party from disaster, continue to guide and comfort us for the next thousand years and for eternity. Please raise your glasses and drink, and let us be silent for a moment before we return to the fray.

Graham Gooch

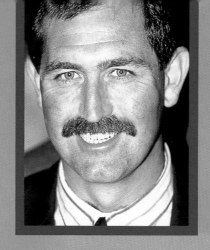

'OK opening batsman and England Tour Manager, 1998/1999.'

guests
Muhammad Ali
Bobby Moore
Donald Bradman
Bobby Charlton
Rowan Atkinson
Barry Richards
Pele
Franz Beckenbauer
Isse Nartion
Jack Nicklaus

(All the above sportsmen are particular heroes of mine.)

location
On the cricket square at the famous Lords cricket ground.

music
Van Morrison: *Live in San Francisco*

toast
May the next 1000 years produce many sportsmen of your calibre.

Pele

Rowan Atkinson

Susan Greenfield

Albert Einstein

Queen Elizabeth I

Kenneth Griffith

Actor Kenneth Griffith was a well respected stage actor before turning to films: 'I have tried to probe the deep truth about human affairs and then communicate what I have discovered. I have seen myself as a first-aid man.

guests William Shakespeare Because of his vision of the human predicament and the words he used.
Fidel Castro His steadfast bravery against the evil elements in the U.S.A.
Jesus Christ I need to know who he truly was.
William Gladstone We British will always need an honest, perceptive leader.
Pericles The giant of principles.
Mozart I owe him more than I can repay.
Tyrone Guthrie A much valued friend whom I sorely miss.
Huw Wheldon As above.
Amy (One of my five children) Because...
Chiara Perretti My last lady-love.
Ernest Griffith My splendid grandfather who was virtually my father.

location Tenby, in South West Wales, where I was born. It is extremely beautiful and is still remarkably peaceful.

menu Fresh lobster from the local sea, home-made ice-cream, good champagne.

seating plan Wherever they choose to sit.

music Mozart's Clarinet Concerto in A Major (K622); Mozart's Piano Concerto No. 21 in C Major (K467).

toast May the new Millennium learn wise lessons from the wretched chaos of the old Millennium.

May the new Millennium learn wise lessons from the wretched chaos of the old Millennium.

Susan Greenfield is Professor of Pharmacology at Oxford and Director of the Royal Institution of Great Britain. She is a world expert on the human brain and is currently preparing a major six-part series on the brain and mind, to be broadcast on BBC2 in the year 2000.

guests
Albert Einstein
Leonardo da Vinci
Queen Elizabeth I
Oscar Wilde
George Bernard Shaw
Orson Welles

location In the piazza of a Mediterranean village as the sun is going down.

menu Feta salad • Curry • Champagne.

music Hits of the 1960s and 1970s.

toast To the individual.

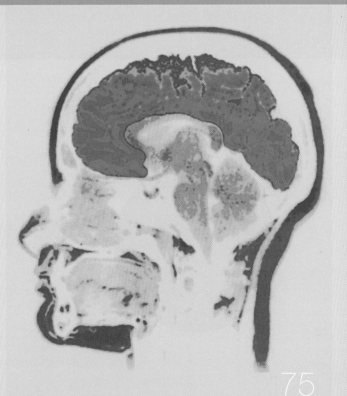

Eric Hall

Lionel Bart One of my favourite English writers, who, again, passed away recently.
Bob Hope A man I was privileged to meet many times.
Queen Mum Another great lady.
That would be a nice mixture, as they are all in the same business (except for my mum, but she loves showbiz). Sinatra was a great singer of people's songs and his favourite writers and some of mine would be there.

menu I'd get a top chef to actually do it properly.

music I've got a piano in my house so it will be nice to have Oscar here, and there would be... not a free for all, not a karaoke, but, you know, he'd just play great piano. And Frank, if he wants to do a few numbers.

location My house, for sure – the only place I'd want to be. I'm a monster egomaniac! Hey, you know I'd go to Marks and Spencer and I'd have my basket full of steaks and things, and they'd say, 'Oh Eric, you're eating well this week – you only normally have about one steak – you've got about twenty steaks there!' And I'd say , 'Well, I'm having dinner tonight with Frank Sinatra and Irving Berlin'.

guests
My lovely mum I'd like her to be there.
Frank Sinatra Lots of monster name-dropping here, as I've met him!
James Cagney One of the greatest actors.
Edward G. Robertson
Irving Berlin I love old songs – he was meant to be one of the greatest songwriters ever.
Oscar Peterson It would be a very showbizzy thing; you've got all those people there – songwriters and singers – so you need a pianist and he is one of the great pianists for me.
Sunny Cahill (film maker) I'd like to have people I've met when they were alive and some who are still alive.

I'm a monster egomaniac!

Frank Sinatra

Leader of the Conservative Party.

William Hague

The Beatles

guests

William Shakespeare For his after dinner stories.

Oliver Cromwell For his lessons in Party discipline.

Cardinal Richelieu To make sure we all say grace.

Elizabeth I To pay for it all.

Nigella Lawson To tell us about the food.

Leonardo da Vinci Because he knows how to paint suppers.

Steve Ovett So I can't be accused of bias.

Meatloaf To sing for us after dinner.

Cilla Black To do the seating plan.

Jim Davidson To tell the jokes.

Ffion Hague For my sanity.

William Shakespeare

Elisabeth I

location I would hold the dinner at the Lake Palace Hotel, Udaipur, where I spent my honeymoon.

menu Roast beef and Yorkshire pudding.

seating plan Leave that up to Cilla Black.

music I would listen to The Beatles, live, of course.

toast The toast would be to a peaceful, prosperous, successful, creative, inclusive and happy new Millennium.

Professional boxer – WBO
Featherweight Champion of the World.

Prince
Naseem Hamed

guests

Me, Eleasha, my wife and Sami, my son
Bruce Lee, Muhammad Ali, Michael Jordan, Jackie Chan
The combination of these legends would not only make for
great conversation but I know we would really enjoy spending
time together.
Chris Tucker, Chris Roch and Lee Evans Pure entertainment
and we would all be in fits of laughter.
All my own and my wife's families No Millennium celebration
would be complete without all our respective families.

location At home – because there's no place like home.

menu Traditional Arabic food (I know a lot of people who can
cook but no one cooks better than my mum) and as we don't drink
alcohol, the bar would consist of exotic fruit cocktails.

music It would be a mix, due to guests' varying tastes; the
compilation would include soul, swing, R&B, and traditional Arabic
music.

toast I want to thank Allah, my friends and family for all of their
support, belief and love. It is the belief and support of others that
makes us better people. As we enter a new Millennium it is a time
to believe in each other more and value the contributions of those
around us. Strive for what you want because if you believe, you
can achieve.

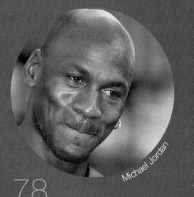

Michael Jordan

Mohammed Ali

no one cooks better than my mum

Nick Hancock

'Ken and Adele Hancock's lad.'
Nick Hancock is a comedian, actor
and presenter of the BBC sports quiz
They think it's all over.

guests
Gordon Banks
John Marsh
Mike Pejic
Mike Barnard
Dennis Smith
Alan Bloor
Terry Conroy
Jimmy Greenhoff
John Ritchie
Peter Doubing
George Eastham
They were Stoke's 1972
League Cup winning side.
(Apologies to John Mahoney,
the substitute, for not finding
room for him.)

location
The site of
the old Victoria ground in
Stoke, which, sadly, did not
make it to the Millennium.

menu
North Staffordshire
oatcakes with melted cheese.
Strong, sweet tea.

seating plan
4:2:4
(Football team configuration)

music
Something by
Jackie Trent.

toast
Let's do better.

Happy Mondays

Bez

guests
Debs and my family
Joe Strummer and his family
Dermot
Danny
Fat neck (three mates)
And any other close friends
and family because it is a
very special time to spend
with special people.

Sean Ryder

guests
Jesus
Commander Catherine
Jane Way (Star Trek)
Randal (deceased) and
Hopkirk – 70s T.V. show
Tom and Jerry
Rowetta
Larry Flint
and every Playboy Bunny Girl
and Penthouse Pet there has
ever been.

Gordon Banks

Jesus

I founded Red or Dead in 1982, after getting my degree. Red or Dead has gone on to win the Streetstyle Designer of the Year award in 1995, 1996 and 1997. I've got 5 fantastic kids, a wonderful wife, and I like football.

Wayne Hemmingway
(Red or Dead)

guests
Gordon Banks
George Cohen
Ray Wilson
Nobby Stiles
Jackie Charlton
Bobby Moore
Alan Ball
Martin Peters
Geoff Hurst
Roger Hunt
Bobby Charlton
THEY WON THE WORLD CUP FOR ENGLAND IN 1966, BEATING THE GERMANS!!!!!!!

seating plan
5:3:2 formation with Wayne Hemmingway sitting on the bench so as not to upset the formation.

G.B

G.C, NS, JC, BM, RW

AB, BC, MP,

GH, RH.

location
The Banqueting Suite, Wembley Stadium, Wembley, Middlesex, England.

menu
Prawn cocktail • steak • egg and chips • spotted dick • Irish Coffee • beer.

music
The Top 30 from Sat 30th July 1966.

toast
To England winning the World Cup in the Millennium we are leaving, and to winning the World Cup many times in the Millennium we are entering.

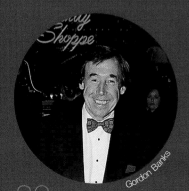
Gordon Banks

George Cohen

Bobby Moore

Bobby Charlton

James Herbert

Bestselling horror writer, James Herbert has sold over 40 million books worldwide in 28 different languages. 'Thin, dark-haired, going grey (but good hair). Enjoy good company, sometimes have a wicked sense of humour, self-contained. Achievements...? Still trying.'

guests

Jesus Christ Need some answers.

Adolf Hitler Need some answers.

Steve McQueen The greatest male star.

John Casavettes Great actor, great director.

Brigitte Bardot She'd give me an adrenaline rush.

John F. Kennedy Would like to discuss how the flesh overwhelmed the spirit.

H.G. Wells Would like to discuss all his work.

Fay Weldon [*host*] Great company and very wise.

Stan Laurel Would raise gentle laughter.

Albert Einstein I'd like to hear more...

Tony Hancock I'd like to cheer him up.

location

My own home; all my dinner parties are great. (And think of the honour if they all stayed over.)

menu

Caviar, oysters, fresh asparagus, lobster, Italian ice-cream, strawberries. Pints of Ruddles, Sea Breezes (vodka, grapefruit juice, cranberry juice, ice), Polish vodka, Armagnac, port.

seating plan

Jesus and Hitler on either side to begin with, but I would move around to have a personal conversation with each and every guest.

music

Music going through the century, from Fred Astaire to Rap and Hip Hop. The split second after midnight I would play Greig's *Morning*.

toast

I'd thank God the old one was behind us and ask him to give us another chance with the new.

all my dinner parties are great

H. G. Wells

John F. Kennedy

Steve McQueen

Brigitte Bardot

81

Richard Herring
(Lee and Herring)

Comedian. In the double act *Lee and Herring.*

guests Stephen Jay Gould A brilliant, entertaining and extremely clever writer on evolution. He would debunk the superstition surrounding the Millennium.

Rasputin He was a cat who was really gone. He liked drinking, fighting and women – a must for any party. It was a shame how he carried on.

Derek Smalls Bass player of Spinal Tap. He would be the lukewarm water to the fire and ice the other guests would represent.

Mike Cosgrave He's my best friend, and I know at least he would talk to me.

Dawn French Because I'd like to snog her at midnight. Plus, she's really funny and genuinely lovely.

T.K. Herring My dad. He would get drunk and tell Rasputin embarrassing stories about me when I was a kid.

Ice T My upbringing in Cheddar was similar to his in south central LA. Maybe we could persuade him to sing one of his pop songs.

Perkin Warbeck My favourite historical character. Pretender to the throne in 1491 – you've got to admire his cheek.

Barbara Herring My mum. I think she'd get on with Ice T. She's the woman of the Millennium.

Tom Parker-Bowles A popular addition to any party. He could get some publicity for us all.

location Pompeii – it is the most wonderful place I have been. The past captured by disaster; a reminder of our achievements and our fragility.

menu Starter: Pickled onion Monster Munch and banana Toffo chew bars. Main course: Fried egg and chips made by my mum. Pudding: Fruit Pastille lollies. To drink, diet Coke or Budvar beer.

seating plan Tom Parker-Bowles sitting at a table on his own (not with the grown-ups).

music *I Am In Love With the World* by The Chicken Shed Theatre. *Kill the Poor* by the Dead Kennedies. The theme song from Morons from Outer Space.

toast As you know, the Millennium is the 2000th anniversary of nothing, as, if Jesus existed, he must have been born in, at latest, 4 BC, whilst Herod was alive. Still, good excuse for a party. Sorry there weren't more girls, Rasputin. Here's to the death of religion and other superstitions and to the birth of humanism and rationality. Anyone for another pack of Monster Munch?

British author and historian.
Author of 50 books.

Christopher Hibbert

Harold Pinter

Joan Collins

guests

The Rev. Sidney Smith
He would make us all laugh.

Mae West She would make us all laugh.

John Betjeman We would ask him to immortalise the feast in verse.

William Hogarth We'd ask him to paint the scene.

Cleopatra Who wouldn't be excited at the thought of seeing her?

Joan Collins [*host*] Because she is gorgeous and amusing.

Antonia Fraser Because she is gorgeous, amusing and clever.

Nell Gwynn Because she is irresistable.

Edward VII Because he'd relish the food and the occasion.

Elizabeth I Because she'd love to meet the King and he her.

Samuel Johnson Because he longed to see Venice and was such a dedicated trencherman.

menu
Asparagus, Dover sole, lemon sorbet, Stilton. Cappucino, whiskey and soda, Sancerre.

music
Handel's Water Music played in gondolas on the Grand Canal, beneath the Gritti Palace windows.

location
The Gritti Palace hotel, Venice.

toast
To the new Millennium in the hope that it will see the fulfilment of the wish of John Ruskin who held it to be 'undisputable that the first duty of a state is to see that every child born therein shall be well housed, clothed, fed and educated till it attains years of discretion.'

Rachel Heyhoe Flint

guests

Kiri te Kanawa A great singer and golfer.
Sir Tim Rice A great lyricist and cricketer.
Baroness Thatcher [*host*] A truly great lady.
John Major A caring prime minister and great cricket buff.
Lord Condrey My cricketing hero.
Seve Ballesteros My golfing hero.
Billy Wright Great England and Wolves footballer (deceased).
Nick Faldo Misunderstood world-class golfer.
Victoria Wood Great comedienne (for after-dinner speech)
Brian Johnston Summers will never be the same without his cricketing commentaries.
Sir Jack Hayward ('Union Jack') British millionaire who saved such ancient relics as SS Great Britain, Lundy Island, and England Women's Cricket Team.

location
Balcony of La Manga Club's Hyatt Regency Hotel, overlooking south course 18th green and palm tree lined fairways. (Our second home is a golf bungalow at La Manga Club).

menu
Typical Spanish menu; paella, anchovies, tapas, fish baked in salt, roll-mop herrings. Rioja from beginning to end.

music
Placido Domingo (and the two other tenors, if available!)

toast
HASTA LA MANANA Here's to tomorrow – I don't like looking back!

John Major

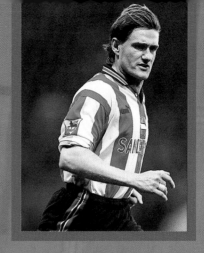

Andy Hinchcliffe

guests

Paul Weller
George Orwell
Quentin Tarantino
Robert de Niro
Winona Ryder
Alan Partridge
Thomas Hardy
Liam Gallagher
Salvador Dali
Malcolm X
Martin Luther-King

location
Stocksbridge bypass, near Sheffield; Yorkshire's very own riviera.

menu
Avocado, mozarella, lobster, sun-dried tomatoes, ciabatta, mushy peas. Coffee and petits-fours. Hobnobs. Château Petrus, Château Margaux, Diet Lilt, plenty of sparkling Vimto.

music
Gustav Holst's *The Planets' Suite*; *Mars* (bringer of war) a particular favourite.

toast
Out with the old, in with the new. Let's get lashed.

Liam Gallagher

Quentin Tarantino

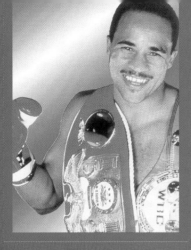

Knight of honour; brave and noble, kind and funny. Welterweight titles: Southern area British Commonwealth European Champion; former two-time World Boxing Champion; IBF World; WBC World; Commonwealth Light Middleweight Champion.

Lloyd Honeyghan

guests **Lauren Hill** Perfect woman, fabulous voice, most gorgeous lips. My ragamuffin queen.

Iman

Rio (the Gladiator) My personal body guard.

Tony Braxton My Nubian Queen, other than Cleopatra.

Grace Jones My sparring partner and body guard.

Mel B (Spice Girl) Strong character. Who knows where she's coming from and where she's going to.

Whitney Houston A woman you can depend on.

?? This space is reserved for a very special lady in my future.

Bianca Honeyghan My daughter who is nine years old. The head of my body guards. Love you, B – my 'Jamaican Girl'.

Grandma Epsie A very good domino player – my partner. She brought me up as her son from the age of twelve months until I was nine years old - my mother.

Grandpa Brown Joe A great inspiration in my life, especially during my days a young boy in Jamaica, when I carried his gun for him when we went duck-shooting down 'Great Pond', Treasure Beach... my happiest years. I love him with all my heart.

location The Bluemountain Hills in Jamaica, by the river. This is how I like to relax each time I am in Jamaica on holiday..

menu Roast fish, curry goat, rice and peas, jerk chicken, fried fish and sami, fish tea, coconut water, mango, sugar cane and water melon. White rum, 'Red Stripe' beer, fruit punch, water.

music Bob Marley: *Three Little Birds* – to christen the new Millennium. Frank Sinatra: *I Did it My Way* – the soundtrack for the evening. Love Star sound system playing reggae music 24 hours, ragamuffin style.

The Honeyz (Naima Belkhiati)

How can I describe myself? Ambitious, independent, friendly and very hard working. My ambitions are yet to be fulfilled but my greatest achievement is the fact that I had a dream and the belief to go after what I wanted.

guests
Yul Brynner
Prince Charles
Mariah Carey
Cary Grant
Billie Holiday
Marilyn Monroe
Lucky Santangelo From Jackie Collins's book, *Lucky*.
Mark McGrath From the band, Sugar Ray.
Adam Sandler
Stephen King
Shakespeare

Mariah Carey

Marilyn Monroe

location The island of St.Barts. It's a private island with beautiful beaches.

toast I would like to have a toast to the future – a better world filled with hope, love and peace.

Shakespeare

Kelly Hoppen

Interior designer.
'Love of order, and an appreciation of quality in all things. Generous friend and companion.'

guests Vicki Quasha She is my best friend in the whole world.
Natasha Corrett She is my daughter and I couldn't be without her.
Ed Miller My husband and soul mate.
James Dean To find out if he is as sexy as he looked in his movies.
Picasso He was one of the most creative minds of the last Millennium and he loved women.
The Dalai Lama It is always good to have a living god at a dinner party.
Richard Gere For his combination of interests and good looks.
Marilyn Monroe An incredible woman.
Elvis Love the way he moves.
Steve Martin One of the funniest men alive.
J. F. Kennedy Jnr Because he was gorgeous!

Picasso

Richard Gere

Dalai Lama

location Bali Amanwana on Moyo Island, Indonesia. Fireworks, incense from all over the world, masses of exotic flowers in huge urns in every corner and hundreds of candles lit.

menu Cristal pink champagne. Caipirhinas. Exotic Balinese foods and fruits and loads of Belgian chocolates. Barrels of Haagon Daz ice-cream – 'praline' and 'cookies 'n' cream' flavour.

music The Beatles playing *Let it Be*, live.

toast To the memory of all those before us, the lessons learned and all the laughter, joy, tenderness and accumulated love of the generations. And to a future where peace and love for our fellow travellers dominates the lives of everyone on the planet.

Steve Martin

The Beatles playing 'Let it Be', live

I am a popular comedian whose other considerable gifts have yet to mature.

Barry Humphries

guests

H.R.H. Prince Charles Warm, witty, intuitive and easily recognised.
Tamara de Lempicka Narcissistic but nice.
Stephen Spender ... who will make us all laugh.
Barbara Amiel (Mrs Conrad Black) Gorgeous and discreetly bright.
Osbert Sitwell One of my favourite authors.
Hedy Lamarr Clever and beautiful and Viennese –
my childhood crush.
Emmanuel Chabriel A life-enhancing composer.
Catherine the Great Naughty but nice.
Steven Issillis Master cellist – joyous companion.
Coral Browne Wicked and wonderful and Australian.
John Betjeman Because I miss him.

location Al fresco, under the giant fig tree at Lady Pru Holden's house, on the beach at Kangaroo Island, South Australia.

menu

Lizzie Spender's (my wife's) spaghetti al putanesca.
Grilled Adelaide whiting.
Salads by Giovanna Toppi of Machiavelli's restaurant, Sydney.
Selection of desserts from the Salopian Inn, McLaren Vale, South Australia.
Portugese cheeses.
Tasmanian wines.

seating plan Constantly moving.

music No music under conversation – it's the height (or depth) of barbarism.

toast The Queen.

Norman Hood

"DON'T KNOW WHO'S ON THIS GUEST LIST, BUT THEY'VE JUST ORDERED ANOTHER DOZEN DEEP-FRIED CHEESEBURGERS!"

Will Hutton

Editor-in-Chief of *The Observer*, author of *The State We're In*, father of 3, books, TV, films, professorship, etc., etc.

guests Cheryl Crow Best woman rock singer ever, and sexy.
John Maynard Keynes Best economist.
William Beveridge Best social theorist.
Richard Tawney Best social democratic theorist.

Adam Smith Love to meet him.
Van Morrison Lifelong worshipper of his music.
Nye Bevan Another hero.
Jane Hutton (and Sarah, Alice and Andrew) Or else she'd never talk to me again.

Marilyn Monroe Need I say more?
Gordon Brown [*host*] Only time we would get to talk properly – and he needs to meet Keynes, Beveridge and Tawney.
Tony Blair And he needs them too.

Van Morrison

Adam Smith

Gordon Brown

Marilyn Monroe

location Garden of a villa on Lake Garda.

menu Endless 'River-Cafe' type canapes • Mushrooms on biocciotta bread • Salmon • Thai Chicken with satay sauce • Ben & Jerry ice-cream, raspberries • Champagne, Chablis, Kingfisher beer, Pina Colada

music Van Morrison and Cheryl Crow.

toast To Our Times. And hoping humanity makes a better job of it over the next 1,000 years than it did over the last 1,000!

Glenda Jackson CBE MP was an actress before entering Parliament and won two Oscars. She has campaigned for the Anti-Apartheid Movement, Amnesty, Oxfam, Shelter and Friends of the Earth. She was appointed Parliamentary Under Secretary of State for Transport in 1997.

Glenda Jackson

The Bilbao Guggenheim

guests Nelson Mandela Who needs a reason?
Fred Astaire There'll be music. We may dance.
Marlon Brando Oh, please!
Mary Robinson A privilege to be in her company.
Greta Garbo She didn't really want to be alone if the company was good.
Betty Boothroyd One of my heroines.
Barbara Castle As above.
Billy Bragg The musician.
Emma Thompson She's a terrific actress.
Bart Simpson Youth conquers all.
William Shakespeare No reason needed.

location The Bilbao Guggenheim, if the new Norman Foster home for the E.L.A isn't quite ready.

menu It's a 'bring your favourite dish' picnic, so it will be a surprise. I'll supply the drink – water, wine, coffee and tea.

seating plan It's a picnic so people will sit where they like.

music Well, if Billy Bragg accepts he'll hopefully play, otherwise 60s Motown.

Marlon Brando

Fred Astaire

Johnny Bravo

guests

Michelle Pfeiffer She's a babe.
Cindy Crawford She's a babe.
Elle McPherson She's a babe.
Cher She's a babe.
Daphne (From Scooby Doo) She's a babe.
Velma (accompanying Daphne. It's that pretty chick, ugly chick thing).
Little Suzy She would come anyway.
Mama Because she's my mama.

location Mom's.

menu Burgers • Mega Pizza • Cola • Me.

seating plan Johnny in the middle surrounded by babes. Oh, and, of course, mom and little Suzy.

music Strictly Rock 'n' Roll with some Barry White and James Brown thrown in for those tender moments.

toast To the man who makes babes go round, life worth living and mirrors blush. I give you Johnny. To be delivered by Johnny.

Ronan Keating (Boyzone)

guests I'd invite everybody – all the children especially. I'd want them to have a good time!

location In the Millennium Dome – we've got to use it for something!

menu Pepsi and McDonalds!

music Westlife.

toast Peace and goodwill to all.

In the Millennium Dome
 – we've got to use it for something!

Grand Master Gary Kasparov was born in 1963 in Baku, Azerbaijan. In 1980 he was the world junior champion, in 1981 the Soviet champion, and in 1985, at the age of 22, the youngest ever world chess champion after defeating Anatoly Karpov

Garry Kasparov

guests

Sir Isaac Newton
Winston Churchill
Napoleon Bonaparte
Leonardo da VInci
Machiavelli
The 5th Earl of Rutland
(William Shakespeare)
Charles Darwin
Voltaire
Abraham Lincoln
Thomas Jefferson

location

Château Margaux.

menu

French cuisine and wine.

music

Mozart's 40th symphony.

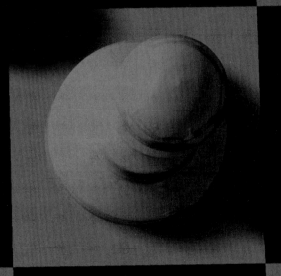

Old Millennium toast

The past is the invention of our predecessors, who looked at this past from different angles and formed their own interpretations, which are not the best for history. This has led to ethnic hatred that perpetuates itself for centuries.

New Millennium toast

To a truly democratic Russia. Take the USA as an example of a country where the government sues its most successful software company and is not sure of winning – can we ever hope for that in Russia?

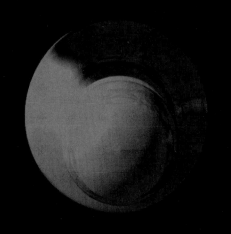

Brian Keenan

Age 48. Lecturer, writer, author. A man who shuns immortality but wants to live forever, travelling the unending road of life.

guests Audrey Doyle (my wife) She radiates charm and hospitality and can effortlessly convert strangers into friends. Rosa Luxembourg For her visionary socialism and feminism. El Greco Whose fabulous paintings made a perfect marriage of humanity, passion and mysticism. Francis Stuart The finest and most European of Irish novelists. Albert Camus For his profound humanity, his masterpieces in literature, and because he died too young. Pablo Neruda For his magnificent opus 'The Canto General' where poetry, history and politics meet. Sor Juana Ines de la Cruz For her passionate and subversive defence of the rights of women to intellectual pursuit. Her intellectual rigour and compassion terrified the Spain of the Inquisition. Erich Fromm For his challenging exploration of the meaning and context of love. Billy Connolly To prevent the conversation from becoming too heavy. Freda Kahlo Painter and wife of Diego Rivera. Their styles of work and of life are so different, so the story of their relationship must be fascinating. Herman Melville For writing *Moby Dick* and the rest of his canon of novels.

location Torres del Paine, Patagonia, Chile. There is no other landscape that has so penetrated the mind and the imagination. Shakespeare, Coleridge, Poe, Donne, Dante...the list is endless. The perfect place to liberate the mind and exorcise the soul.

seating plan With me as the observer, my wife as the genial host and Billy Connolly's ribald humour at the centre, I have mixed the living with the dead, and male with female, in a mix that might take conversation long into the wee hours and unearth remarkable confessions.

toast The past is merely a set of incidents that have brought us to this point. Tomorrow history will pass away. We may find ourselves on a point of departure when 'hope and history' might finally rhyme. Thus we might walk out of the confines of history, create anew and live within the vision that is within us all.

Dick King-Smith

'Lazy schoolboy, accident prone soldier, failed farmer, second-rate salesman, unremarkable factory worker, innumerate schoolteacher. Now (happily) a children's author and head of a large and still burgeoning family.'

Marian Keyes

At the age of 30, dealt with alcoholism and went on to write four novels in five years: *Watermelon*, *Lucy Sullivan is Getting Married*, *Rachel's Holiday*, and *Last Chance Saloon*.

guests Holly Golightly from *Breakfast at Tiffanys*. She's edgy, interesting and fascinatingly tormented.
Michael Bywater The journalist. He's highly entertaining and seems like a compassionate, nice person.
My granny, Katie Cotte She was a great raconteur and had lovely, no-nonsense values.
Gore Vidal He's articulate, ascerbic, incredibly clever and has an astonishingly clear sighted grasp of our world.
Grace O'Malley Irish pirate queen from the sixteenth century. She could tell us a thing or two about girl power.
Jesus Christ a) it's his birthday. b) there are a lot of questions I'd like answers to!
Mary Robinson UN High Commissioner for Human Rights. In my opinion, man's inhumanity to man is the greatest scourge of the human condition. She's trying to curb the terrible things we do to one another.
Eddie Izzard Because he's a hoot and as surreal as they come.
Kathy Burke The actress. She seems to be outrageously funny and yet very warm.
Gandhi He can give us lessons in how to be nice to each other.
Harrison Ford Circa 1984 in *Working Girl*. For his personality, of course!

location On the wide, golden, salty-aired beach at Lahinch, Co. Clare, Ireland, within earshot of the crashing waves. We'd need a lot of bonfires, and a stand-by marquee in case it rained, though!

menu To drink we'd have Guinness, Black Velvets, Irish whisky. To eat we'd start with oysters and Irish smoked salmon on soda bread, followed by chowder made from locally caught fish and shellfish – mussels and scallops etc. For our main course we'd have bacon and cabbage (but of course) or freshly caught salmon, accompanied by roast parsnips, carrots, and about twenty different varieties of potato (sauteed, roast, mashed, dauphinoise, pancakes, rosti...I could go on and on). All very traditional and not a coulis in sight! For dessert we'd have apple tarts, trifles and sponge cakes made by the local mammies. We'd finish with tea so strong the spoon can stand up in it, and chocolate covered Kimberly biscuits (a uniquely Irish confection). In proper Irish fashion we'd have about 15 times too much food and everything would (hopefully) taste even better than usual because of being eaten in the briny air.

guests Cardinal Hume (to say Grace). The gentlest of gentleman.
Shakespeare The greatest of writers.
Judi Dench My favourite actress.
David Attenborough Best of natural history presenters.
King Charles II My great, great, great, great, great, great, great, great grandfather.
Anna Ford Most decorative.
Anthony Trollope My favourite author.
William Esau Heard My great grandfather, who lived to 102 and three quarters.
Jane Austen My favourite authoress.
Boadicea One tough lady.
Beatrix Potter In a class of her own.

location The Island of Mayreau in the Caribbean.

menu Smoked salmon and scrambled eggs, jam roly poly, Stilton. Some good Chablis, and some good Claret.

music The Beatles (*Sergeant Pepper* Album), Mozart (*The Jupiter* symphony).

toast Here's to the Old Millennium with all its wonders and all its 'horrors'! On balance I'm glad to see the back of you. As to the new Millennium, the best of happiness and good luck to my children, my grandchildren, and my great-great grandchildren (shan't last to see a great-great grandchild). May man's inhumanity to man begin to lessen.
Do as you would be done by. Cheers.

Neil Kinnock

Moses

Abraham Lincoln

Ava Gardner

guests

Moses For views on leadership and feeding people in difficult conditions.

Abraham Lincoln For fascinating words and dry jokes.

George Orwell For challenging thoughts on the past and the future.

Charles Dickens For great stories, brilliantly told.

Elizabeth Barrett Browning To recite her own poems.

Dolores 'Barrur' – La Passionara. Revolutionary, war heroine and a hell of a woman.

Dorothy Parker The greatest ever supper table sage and gossip.

Duke Ellington For music and cool talk.

Ava Gardener To look at and listen to.

Aung San Suu Kyi So she has a meal in real safety for the first time in years.

Rory Bremner For friendship and so that he can impersonate any absentees.

location On a large yacht sailing around the coast of Wales. At the Millennium hour I wouldn't be able to see the land but I'd know it was there.

menu A large selection of British traditional food from steak 'n' kidney pie to fish 'n' chips with supplements from India (courtesy of a Nepalese chef) and Mexico. 'Brains' beer from Cardiff, a really fine Chablis, some rich Burgundy and a selection of malt whiskies.

music Beethoven, Bruchner and Bruch selections; the whole of Shostakovich's Gadfly Suite; Rock 'n Roll 1955-1970; items from Treovchy Male Voice Choir and the band of the Welsh Guards (for a sing-a-long); Duke Ellington live.

toast Toast the progress made and the beauty created despite the conflict and cruelty of past Millennia – and greet a coming Millennium by striving for peace, prosperity and liberty, everywhere on the planet.

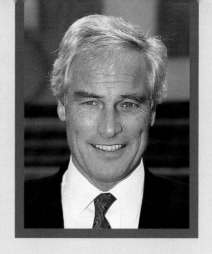

I suppose I'm a writer and broadcaster. From 1966 to 1974 I was a university lecturer, then from 1974 to 1986 I was an MP for Labour … and I have been presenting *Kilroy*, made by my own company, since 1986 – the longest running daytime television talk show.

Robert Kilroy-Silk

David Beckham

Oliver Cromwell

Marilyn Monroe

guests

Thomas Hobbes The greatest English political philosopher.

Oliver Cromwell The greatest Englishman.

Truman Capote

Anthony Crossland He was Foreign Secretary in the last Labour government. Extremely urbane and droll, and a philosopher too. Someone whom I knew and liked and who I voted for in the Labour leadership contest that Michael Foot won – he lost with Dennis Healey. He is probably the most influential person in British politics on political philosophy in the contemporary period.

William Silk My 23-year-old father who was killed in action in the Royal Navy in the last war, and whom I never met.

David Beckham The only real world-class footballer we've ever had… ever, that is.

Sidney My black Labrador who died last year and who I would like to sit by the side of the gathering.

Niccolo Machiavelli Because I'm looking for interesting political, philosophical and general conversation, and he's well versed and rounded, cynical and sharp. He knows about human nature and can see into people and see behind what they're saying. He would complement everyone else.

Dirk Bogarde Because he used to own the house that I lived in and that I now own in England; he wrote about it quite extensively and had lots of good and entertaining times there with people like Kate Kendall and Judy Garland. I also think he's quite amusing in his own right and he writes a lot, so he could tell me about the good things.

Marilyn Monroe Because she was the sexiest woman in the world.

Catherine Deneuve Because she's the most beautiful woman in the world and she would add to the glamour. That sounds a bit sexist but I think they would both have a lot to contribute; and they would unsettle things a bit – create a bit of a diversion.

location

At my house in the mountains, in Spain – in the evening, in the open air, on a big, open table, overlooking the views down to Africa, with the mountains down behind us.

menu

Foie gras; Caviar; Cyrano ham (from the black pigs in Spain); Roast beef and Yorkshire pudding; Black figs from Spain and white grapes.

Start with a Charles Heidsieck champagne – 1985; then move on to Louis Roederer – 1985; finish with a Petite Liquorelle, which is a Moët et Chandon liqueur. (They've stopped making it and now you can't get it, but my daughter managed to get hold of the last few crates for me). And obviously no one else likes it so it can't be much good!…but at least it would be kind of unusual; and a Walls 1980 port.

music

Fleetwood Mac and Tom Waites.

Perhaps a bit before and a bit after the meal, but not during it. We don't want a distraction- there will be too much to talk about.

Maggie Koumi

56 year-old editor of *Hello!* magazine. Married. Able to work 48 hours without food or snooze. Chainsmoker. Biggest achievement is still being alive.

guests

Wallis Simpson For all the gossip on the royals.

Jackie Kennedy Onassis For all the gossip on the Kennedys.

Florence Nightingale In case of emergencies.

Bette Davis To throw a theatrical tantrum.

Phoebe of *Friends* For totally incongruous light relief.

Oscar Wilde To tell us a bedtime story.

Harry Enfield To make up for all the other characters that can't be there.

Dirty Harry In case things get out of hand.

Nat King Cole To serenade us with that sweet, sweet voice.

Jesus To discover the truth, once and for all.

Ramon Sola, my husband. Because he'd kill me if I didn't!

location

Botswana, Africa. To watch the sunset and the sunrise in the most stunning sky and setting in the world.

menu

A hot buffet of every conceivable bread, pie, and pudding, and lots of crispy chips. Champagne, tea, water. Unlimited supply of cigarettes.

toast

seating plan

If everyone conformed to their roles as we know them, conversation should be hallucinatory.

music

Immortal adagios from Albinoni, Francois de Bois Vallée, Samuel Barber and all the 'Golden Oldies'.

Come fill the cup
What boots it to repeat
How time is slipping
Underneath our feet
Unborn tomorrow
and Dead yesterday
Why fret about them
If today be sweet.

Omar Khayyam

Bette Davis

Clint Eastwood aka Dirty Harry

Harry Enfield

Lisa Kudrow aka Phoebe of Friends

Harold Kroto

A scientist (Nobel prize for chemistry, 1996) whose main interest is graphic art and design. Chairman of Vega Science Trust which produces culturally and intellectually based science programmes for TV and the Internet.

guests **Richard Teyberan** A man who looked at the world and saw it as it was. A great scientist.
Harold Pinter A great writer who sees human beings for what they are.
Salman Rushdie A writer who tests the limits of human thought.
Cat Stevens A former songwriter who now believes people should be put to death for writing a book.
Charlton Heston A former actor who thinks that guns are good for you and me.
Benjamin Rotbladt A scientist who resigned from the Manhattan project when Germany capitulated and there was no longer a nuclear threat.
The Pope To explain to Cat Stevens why he should follow him (the Pope) rather than Allah.
Leonardo da Vinci The greatest scientist/artist of all.
Woody Allen Who can see the serious aspects of life and delineate them with precient wit.
Elizabeth I A woman who really did change the world.
Mahatma Gandhi The greatest pacifist of them all.

music Before midnight: Mahler's 4th Symphony. At midnight: *Journey of the Sorceror* by The Eagles. After midnight: *Imagine* by John Lennon (words only).

toast A toast to the old Millennium in which the intellectual and cultural advances in science, technology and the arts have enabled many to become free of the slavery of working merely to survive, and to have time to pursue interests which will further enhance the humanitarian achievements of the human race. A toast to the new Millennium in which we shall be further freed from outdated mystical philosophies which continue to differentiate and divide segments of the human race in the name of patriotism, religious conviction and colour.

Ian Lang

guests
The Princess Royal
Voltaire
George Washington
She
Leonardo da Vinci
Cleopatra
Peter the Great
Winston Churchill
Lucrezia Borgia
Alexander the Great

location
In a palazzo in the Umbrian hills.

music
Bach, Vivaldi, Purcell, Delius and a little Mozart.

Lord Lang of Monkton was President of the Board of Trade in John Major's Government. He now sits in the House of Lords.

Prue Leith

Writer, cook, business woman and general enthusiast.

guests Sidney Smith
Witty, worldly, wise.
Georgiana, 18th-century Duchess of Devonshire
They would have got on like a house on fire.
Debbo, Duchess of Devonshire As above with above.
Nelson Mandela and **F. W. de Klerk** Great South Africans and great politicians who have not had enough time to sit on a terrace.

Carla Kitt Because Nelson Mandela is an old flirt and would have loved her.
And that's enough. Six or seven for supper is about right because then you can have one conversation and include everybody.

location On a terrace in any South African vineyard in Franschoells Cape. Because it will be warm, beautiful and outside.

menu Barbecued spicy chicken; Pumpkin and garlic mash; Tomato and basil salad; Guava ice-cream; Dom Perignon for the toast; Cape wines for the supper.

seating plan Informally, on the grass or terrace.

music None. Just sounds of the Cape night; toads croaking and crickets.

toast To the old who mostly did their best. To the young who will do better.

To the old who mostly did their best

To the young who will do better

Nelson Mandela

Left to right: Jeremy Dyson, Steve Pemberton, Mark Gatiss, Reece Shearsmith: 'We are a comedy team. Between us we all passed cycling proficiency except one, who has a half-mile swimming badge still sewn onto his trunks. We are now on the telly.'

League of Gentlemen

guests **Christopher Lee**
A great man who, although best known for horror films, has a great voice – see his recent recording of *Wandrin' Star*.
Jimmy Saville A wise man whose road traffic teachings have stayed with us since the early '70s.
'The Duchess' Family name of Jimmy Saville's mum. We would ask her what Jimmy was like as a kid.
Peter Wyngarde A real ladies man who brings a dash of style to any dinner party.
Neil Sedaka The New York songbird, cruelly referred to as the 'disco doughboy'. Great duet with Christopher Lee.
The abominable Dr Phibes The deranged and horribly disfigured doctor would wreak revenge on any round the table who wronged him.
Denise Robertson The agony aunt of Richard and Judy's *Good Morning*. Known for her kindly advice and white hair.

Sir Ernest Shackleton A braver man than Scott, who never got the breaks; a bloody good bloke.
Dick Emery as 'College – the Posh Tramp'. Always a smile and a *bon mot* in the face of life's *travailles*.
Inspector Frederick Abbeline To ask him, 'Who was Jack the Ripper?', and did he like Michael Caine's portrayal of him?
Omega, first of the Time Lords Beneath his mask, there is nothing left of him, save his will. So more food for the rest of us.

location Piz Gloria, the Swiss Restaurant cum allergy clinic atop a snowy mountain, as seen in *On Her Majesty's Secret Service*.

menu Gazpacho to start, or bruschetta with vine tomatoes.
Vesta beef risotto or trout with new potatoes and fresh garden peas.
Crème Brûlée. Elderflower champagne or Dandelion and Burdock.

music Serenaded with 40s Hollywood musical standards by the cast of *It Ain't Half Hot, Mum!*. Don Estelle's *Stella by Starlight* is something else.

toast The Old: That went quick. The New: Here's to swimming with bow-legged women.

The New Toast: Here's to swimming with bow-legged women

Sir Ernest Shackleton (right)

Kathy Lette

A Girl's Night Out

guests **Dorothy Parker** ...who disproves the theory that women aren't funny (I think men always say this because they're terrified of what it is we're being funny about. They think we spend the entire time talking about the length of their penises. Which is not true... because we also talk about the width, which, after childbirth, is much more important.

Becky Sharp The Madonna of her day, flaunting tradition and challenging sexual mores. Okay, she had a few minor faults: snobbery and sexual kleptomania (Becky climbed the social ladder, lad by lad); husband-hunting (she wasn't interested in Mr Right, but Lord, Sir, Marquis Right, at the very least)... but we're talking 1810. With no vote, no union, no fixed wage, no welfare, no contraception...what options were available to women? Apart from factory work, governessing or domestic service, it was prostitution or marriage. (Often a tautology in those days.) A 'fallen woman'...or was she pushed?

Mae West ...who disproved the notion that as a woman it was considered stupid to be too clever. In a man's world, she had what it took to take what they had. As well as being an all-round goddess, Mae was a civil libertarian who went to jail in defence of freedom of expression.

Oscar Wilde An honorary girl whose wit (drier than an AA clinic) should have been registered at police headquarters as a lethal weapon.

Simone de Beauvoir ...who taught us that women didn't have to be Human Handbags draped decoratively over the arm of some Knight in Shining Armani; that we could stand on our own two stilettos; that we should be treated as equals and not sequels; that we were more than just a life-support system to an ovary.

Germaine Greer A Femocet missile, homing in on strategic misogynists and destroying them. Has a healthy dose of sceptic-semia.

Madonna An amorous philanthropist with an irresistible mix of sexuality and self-mockery. At a time when men are still going for gold in the Hypocrisy Olympics (it helps to remember that 'slut', 'whore', 'trollop', 'tramp' are just words used to describe a woman who has the sexual appetite of a man), how liberating to meet a female whose idea of fidelity is to only have one man in bed at a time. Madonna has a chequered present.

Bette Midler (The Divine Miss M) A woman who gives good hedonism.

Jane Austen ...who lived at a time when wedlock was little more than a padlock. Women were meant to be no more than decorative or domestic. Austen's domesticity was limited to the barbecuing of sacred cows - entire herds.

Roseanne Barr's character in the sitcom, *Roseanne.* A woman who goes straight for the jocular vein. When you're at that stage of motherhood where you're putting the kids under the sink and the lethal household substances within your own reach, Roseanne's a reminder that any mother who says she copes all the time is either lying or taking a lot of drugs. She's an antidote for those hideous Stepford Mums - you know, those women who have the ability to discuss their babies' bowel movements long after your own interest has waned.

Emmeline Pankhurst So she can see what she tied herself to the railings for.

Mae West... in a man's world she had what it took to take what they had

The Chippendales

Madonna

location The Chippendales changing room would be nice. We'll have the traditional 'Girl's Night Out' – you know, where you lie to each other that you look great in stretch lycra, swap mascara de-blobbing techniques, compare breasts (whose are biggest) and bottoms (whose have dropped) and stretch marks ('you think yours are bad...'), acupuncture your nostril with a minuscule umbrella every time you take a sip of a cocktail whose name is spiked with an innuendo you're drunk enough to find funny, discuss male partners' anatomical details at length – or not (this is what is meant by 'small talk') – only to regain consciousness twenty-four hours later in the jockstrap of a spent Gladiator.

menu Vintage Champers, Créme Brûlée, and Death by Chocolate, because skinniness is NOT next to godliness. In the 1990's women won't even cook with thick-bottomed sauce pans. They drink skimmed water. Where do they keep their internal organs? In their handbags?

seating plan It doesn't matter where we sit, 'cause we'll all be talking simultaneously anyhow.

music As it's a 'Girl's Night Out', it'll have to be really naff leaping-about-the-room-singing-into-your-hairbrush-type-music like *Sisters Are Doin' it For Themselves*, *We are Family*, *I Got All My Sisters with me*, *I Will Survive*, and *It's Raining Men* (especially backstage at the Chippendales).

The Levellers

A renaissance man trapped in the body of a waster.

Jeremy Cunningham

guests Bobby Sands
IRA hunger striker, also a brilliant
songwriter and democratically
elected MP. Died for what he
believed in. I wonder how many
of our politicians would do that?
Giotto Pre-Renaissance
Italian painter. I'd like to talk to
him about his frescoes – he's
a big influence on me as a
painter.
Joe Strummer The Clash
frontman and my inspiration to
pick up a guitar in the first
place. He played piano on the
Levellers song, *Just the One*,
and was an all-round diamond
geezer.
Saint Columba I'm obsessed
with early Irish history. Columba
was a 6th-century prince who
accepted exile for his Christian
beliefs – putting his money
where his mouth was, like
Bobby Sands.
Sid Vicious I'm a bass player,
and am still a punk...we'd have
a lot to talk about.

Hubert Selby Junior Author
who wrote *Last Exit to Brooklyn*,
amongst other things. Very
interesting man, again, money
where his mouth is.
Willem De Kooning American
abstract Expressionist painter.
Like Giotto, a big influence on
my art. Could talk B and Q
brushes all night long.
Saint Patrick Roman Briton
captured by Irish slave-raiders.
Later escaped, became a
bishop and returned to Ireland
to convert the northeast. His
legacy has been much
manipulated and abused – a
very interesting man, I'm sure.
Dr David Howlett Specialist in
Latin literature of the early
Middle Ages, particularly Irish. A
genius.
Neil Young Songwriter. The
Levellers have supported him a
lot and he's a good bloke.
Woodstock and all that stuff...
Nicky Warman A girl I fancied
when I was 16/17 years old, at
art college, but never had the
bottle to ask out. Still haunted...

location Metway bar, the Hope Tavern – best venue in town.

menu Vegetarian Indian food. Any drink goes. Metway has it all.

music Oasis – Live Forever (of course!)

toast

An ignominious **birth**
A glorious **life**
And a ludicrous **death**

Joe Strummer

Sid Vicious

Monica Lewinsky

guests

Prince Charming
J. Alfred Prufrock
Bridget Jones [*host*]
Sigmund Freud
Ashley Raines (friend)
Willy Wonka
Neysa DeMann Erbland (friend)
Catherine Allday Davis (friend)
William Shakespeare
Mike Lewinsky (brother)
Buster Keaton

location The top of the Eiffel Tower.

seating plan Round table sitting
clockwise: Me, Prince Charming, J. Alfred
Prufrock, Bridget Jones, Sigmund Freud,
Ashley Raines, Willy Wonka, Neysa
DeMann Erbland, Catherine Allday Davis,
William Shakespeare, Mike Lewinsky,
Buster Keaton.

music Abba, the Dave Matthews
Band, my mom singing *My Little Monka*,
Frank Sinatra, Prince, Tracy Chapman,
soundtrack from Guys and Dolls, Jude,
R.E.M, Sara McLachlan, *Build Me Up
Buttercup*, Sting.

toast May there be peace, happiness,
love, laughter, understanding, acceptance,
gratitude, cures for all illnesses and the
means to always take care of the children
in this world, from the first day of the new
Millennium until the end of time. (I'm sure
Shakespeare's toast will be better!!)

menu
Yummies:
My dad's wild mushroom risotto
My dad's Chinese chicken salad
My dad's corn chowder
My dad's filet mignon with Cabernet
reduction sauce
My dad's linguine with mint, tomatoes
and feta
My dad's crepes with Haagen-Dazs
Dulce de Leche
Suzi Q's
Ben and Jerry's Mint Cookies ice-cream
and Doonesberry sorbet
Haribo gummy bears
Benes from anywhere in New Orleans
Cheetos
Brownies from Frank's

Drinks:
Veuve Cliquot
Cosmopolitans
Apple Martinis
Cakebread Chardonnay
Strawberry milkshakes from In and
Out Burger
Ice blended mochas from Coffee Bean
and Tea Leaf
Diet Coke (from the fountain)

Buster Keaton

103

Lennox Lewis

Heavy-weight boxer Lennox Lewis was born in London and grew up in Canada. He won Olympic gold in Seoul in 1988, and later returned to England, turned professional and won the British Heavyweight, Commonwealth and European titles. He was crowned the WBC Heavyweight Champion of the World in 1993 and again in 1997.

Lauren Hill

Nelson Mandela

Muhammad Ali

"I ONLY ASKED HIM WHERE THE PUNCH WAS!"

guests Muhammad Ali
President Nelson Mandela
Doreen and Neville Lawrence
Lauren Hill
Marcus Garvey
Captain Kirk (William Shatner) 'Cause I'm a sci-fi fan.
Madame Curie Through her sacrifice many benefited from penicillin.
Mary Seacole The unsung hero of the Crimean war.

location On the beach in Negril, Jamaica or Waikiki beach in Hawaii.

menu Plenty of healthy portions of ackee, saltfish, chicken and salads, but no pork. I'd stick to natural fruit juices but might allow myself to indulge in the odd glass of Cristal champagne, and rum punch.

music Sly and Robbie, Bob Marley, Lauren Hill, Wu Tang Clan.
Soul classics like Aretha Franklin, James Brown and Marvin Gaye.

toast Let's toast the next thousand years to rebuilding the family unit and the community.

Patrick Lichfield

Royal photographer, the Earl of Lichfield has photographed many famous people and places around the world.

guests

Queen Elizabeth I
Admiral Lord Anson
Jane Digby
David Lean
Joyce Grenfell

C. B. Fry
Lady Diana Cooper
Anethelme Brillat-Savarin
Dame Edna Everage [*host*]
Lord Byron
Kay Kendall

location Tower of the Winds, Shugborough, Staffordshire – ancestral home of the 5th Earl of Lichfield.

seating plan Lord Lichfield is seated to the right of Elizabeth I and the table plan follows in a clockwise direction around to Kay Kendal who would be sitting on Lord Lichfield's right.

Laurence Llewelyn-Bowen

The *Changing Rooms* designer who makes all the girls cry.

guests Margot Ledbetter For a touch of suburban glamour.
Sir Peter Paul Rubens Great after-dinner stories.
Cerys Matthews Earthy conversation and Celtic humour.
John Wilmot, Earl of Rochester Alcoholic, poetic cabaret.

Anthea Turner Because she's great.
The Dalai Lama Amusing and unusual.
Xenobia, Queen of Palmyra Boadicea couldn't make it.
Sir Cecil Beaton For the gossip.
Muriel Spark To record the surrealism of the occasion.

Kit Marlowe
My wife To pull the whole thing together.

location The painted hall at Greenwich Naval College – just the right scale.

menu Prawn cocktail. Doner kebabs. Trifle.

music Purcell, Catatonia, Bach, and Robbie Williams.

toast Here we go again.

Ben de Lisi

Ben de Lisi grew up in Long Island, New York, and later studied at the Pratt Institute of Art, New York. He started his own company in 1984, and won the Glamour Designer of the Year award 1994 and 1995. He opened his first shop in Belgravia in December, 1998.

guests

Angelica Huston I have always found her to be a strong, beautiful and intense woman.

Lucille Ball She has to be one of the world's most funny comics.

Truman Capote For his intellect, vocabulary, charm and bitchiness.

John Travolta For his talent and sex appeal to all people.

Sam Sheppard He is singularly the most sexy man alive.

Jeffrey Boloten My boyfriend who is also sexy, and my partner in life.

Debbie Lovejoy My business partner, best friend, muse and driving force.

Alex Sutton Debbie's boyfriend, who I have grown to love.

Julia Lister Very close friend from Yorkshire, whose humour and kindness knows no bounds.

Stephen Lister Otherwise known as 'Harpic', Julia's husband, who makes us all laugh.

Lilly Savage She'll keep us hysterical.

location
A fantastic decadent palazzo in Venice, on the Grand Canal.

menu
Stuffed baby veal with capers, tomatoes and garlic. Grilled chicken in Marsala with spring onions. Tuff lobster platters. Chargrilled exotic vegetables, polentone. Sweet shards, apples of fennel, mushroom, mozzarella with basil and pine nuts. Venetian cakes. Endless amounts of blinis.

toast
To all our friends and families I wish happiness, peace, good health and success. I hope our journey ahead will be exciting, prosperous, challenging and full of laughter. We should bring with us the knowledge that we have each made our own individual mark on the 20th century, and have had the fortune to have felt love, touched hearts and healed pain. I am in awe of all of you because of what you have given me first, and I am thrilled and proud to be together with you on this most incredible night. Happy New Year!

Angelica Huston... strong, beautiful and intense woman

Cellist

Julian Lloyd Webber

guests

Buddy Holly King of the hiccup!

Edward Elgar Great composer.

William Lloyd Webber
My father, who I'd like to see again.

Elvis The King

Angela Bassett Obvious.

Tommy Taylor Leyton Orient football club
manager.

Dmitri Shostakovich The
last Millennium's greatest composer.

David Lloyd Webber
My seven year-old son.

My girlfriend

Mohammed

Jesus

location
Bali H'ai in the South Pacific
(fictional). The first place the sun rises.

menu
Local wild boar and Fuller's
London Pride.

seating plan
Long table with
guests seated along one side only. From
left to right: William Lloyd Webber, Tommy
Taylor, Mohammed, Jesus, my girlfriend,
myself, Angela Bassett, Edward Elgar,
Dmitri Shostakovich, David Lloyd Webber,
Elvis, Buddy Holly.

music
The soundtrack to *South Pacific*!

toast
Up the O's!

Mohammed

David Lloyd

England cricket coach; keen, but not very good fisherman; horse-racing enthusiast but failed punter; wine and whisky collector who cannot afford it.

guests Andrew Wingfield-Digby Friend, organiser, and example to all.
Will Wingfield-Digby Nephew of Andrew, and good egg.
John Barclay Friend, confidant, supporter and top fisherman.
'Pumper' Pyman Friend whom I see once a year.
Michael Atherton Friend, great company. England T and T.
Eddie Pimlott Best friend, local butcher, golf partner. Former Captain of Cheadle Hulme C.C.

Malcolm Ashton England cricket scorer. Great company.
Cliff Richard Never met him, but seem to have stayed young with him.
Douglas Smith What a terrific man!

music John Lee Hooker and Friends, Van Morrison, Englands Glory (*Jerusalem, Land of Hope and Glory*).

toast I am so pleased that everyone could come; friendship is the most precious thing we possess.

Cliff Richard

Lolly

guests Janet Jackson - she's my idol.

location In my flat - I love it. It's right in the centre of London, so you'd be able to see all the fireworks, which'd be cool.

menu I'd be drinking Rose champagne and Woo-woo's - my favourite cocktail.

music *The Best Things in Life are Free* by Janet Jackson; Luther Vandross; The Des'ree album; My album

toast Love life, turn your music up dead loud, and shout

I love it, I love it!

I am an exceptionally lucky person, paid to write and talk about cricket, blessed with a flourishing family and lacking only time to fit in as much as I should like, and to master the art of going round any golf course in fewer than 80 strokes.

Christopher Martin Jenkins

guests **Jesus** He would approve of saving the children.
Buddha Buddha's conversation and reminiscences with Jesus would be enlightening.
Mohammed Preached much the same disciplines and believed in the same eternal God.
Shakespeare How would one stop him talking? Or would he, like more than one genius, be shy?
Julie Christie In her glorious prime. She strikes me as being intelligent as well as stunningly beautiful.
Henry VIII The virtues of his various wives and advisers, his views on tennis and on the abolition of capital punishment would all be enlightening.
W.G. Grace I have talked too much cricket in my life, but there would be much to learn from him.
Francesca Annis Also in her prime, please; we cannot let Miss Christie have it all her own way.
Samuel Johnson His knowledge would dazzle, his conversation sparkle and he would bring a critical mind to everything.
Brian Johnston Because the evening would be fun with him around and I'd like to hear all the old jokes again!
My wife Judy Lest I should feel just a little out of my depth!

I have been lucky enough to actually have the opportunity to create my own personal 'fantasy feast' for the Millennium. *Reach for the Stars*, my Millennium event, will be taking place in Val d'Isère, high up in the French Alps, one of my very favourite places in the world. Apart from being a huge celebration in itself, this is a Millennium party with a difference. Together with the International Committee of the Red Cross, I am bringing a variety of groups of underprivileged children from different countries of the world to Val d'Isère to celebrate with me.

Vanessa Mae

So, of course, these **children** will be the most important guests at my 'fantasy feast'. I would love to see **Nicolo Paganini** and **Jascha Heifetz** there (two of the greatest violinists who ever lived), as well as **Henry Dunant**, who effectively founded the International Committee of the Red Cross in 1863.

menu Well, given the International nature of my guests, I would like them each to present a dish from their home country. I would also insist that my grandmother cook a feast of her native Singaporean cuisine, which cannot be beaten. As we are in France, perhaps a little foie gras too!

109

John Maynard Smith

Professor of Microbial evolution. 'I have spent my life thinking about evolution; I have watched animals ever since I can remember. I cultivate my garden and I have been married for almost 60 years.'

Mary Shelley

H. G. Wells

guests Olaf Stapledon His *Last and First Men* is the best history of the next hundred million years.

Arthur C. Clarke Another historian of the future.

Charles Darwin Had the best idea anyone ever had.

H.G.Wells His books formed my imagination.

J. B. S. Haldane, my teacher. I think *Possible Worlds* contains the best scientific essays ever written.

Mary Shelley The first science fiction writer?

Ursula le Guin *The Left Hand of Darkness* is perhaps the best science fiction love story.

Anne McLaren I shared a lab with her when she was learning to fertilise mouse eggs in a watch glass.

Rosalind Franklin I have often wondered what she was like.

Elizabeth Bennet I have been in love with her since I was sixteen.

Sheila Maynard Smith, my wife. I would not enjoy the party without her.

location Guarda in the Swiss Engadine. I have had many summer holidays there and would love to see it in the snow.

menu Steak of Tyrannosaurus Rex washed down with the wine we make from grapes grown in our Sussex garden, followed by local nut torte.

music None. I want to hear what people say.

toast To a future in which people forget their differences of race, religion and language and remember their common humanity. To homo sapiens - may he indeed be wise.

Miss Piggy

guests Moi would extend an invitation to the following:

Kermit the Frog Kermit is Moi's one and only love. Besides, Moi must have someone to help out with everyone's coats.

Cleopatra Moi has always wanted to find out who designed her outfits.

Cary Grant What a charmer!

Marie Antoinette Knowing how she feels about cake, she'll probably bring along a yummy dessert.

The Beatles Moi am counting them as 'one'. And no, Yoko can't come.

Tarzan Everyone always says he's a 'real swinger'.

Frank Sinatra 'Old Blue Eyes' - but when he was young 'Old Blue Eyes'.

Princess Grace Her very name oozes grace.

Elvis Presley But he won't be admitted if he's wearing a studded jumpsuit.

William Shakespeare Especially if he looks like Joseph Fiennes.

Ed Sullivan He'll be in charge of the introductions.

location In a customised 747, so we can keep flying over the International Dateline, thus celebrating the New Year over and over again.

menu Oh, what wouldn't we eat? The menu would be planned and prepared by a team of top chefs... with a generous emphasis on dessert.

music As far as music is concerned, we have Sinatra, Elvis and The Beatles at the table. I'm feeding them, so the least they can do is sing a few tunes.

toast As we all gather together on the eve of a new Millennium, facing new challenges, new thrills and new adventures, let us raise our glasses - to Moi! And the rest of vous too. Now if you could all chip in a few dollars, Moi would appreciate it. This banquet cost a fortune!

Moi am counting them as 'one' And no, Yoko can't come.

Cary Grant

Frank Sinatra

The Beatles

Moby

Also known as 'Voodoo Child', Moby is a versatile musician who gained recognition in the early 1990s for his contribution to rap, dance and techno music.

guests Jesus Christ I would like to know if he is, in fact, God, and what this means, and what he thinks about the last 2000 years, and what the universe was like twelve billion years ago, and how big the universe is and what other life is like in the universe etc.
Adolf Hitler I would be curious to know whether he's crazy or unfathomably evil. I've never met anyone who's comfortable with barbarous cruelty, so I'd be interested to get his perspective.
Vincent Van Gogh I like his art. He seems like an insightful guy and he might have some good questions for the other guests.
Pol Pot See Hitler, and I'd like to know what he hoped to accomplish by killing off a third of Cambodia.
Siddhartha Gautama (Buddha) I'd like to see what he and Christ have to say to each other, and he and Pol Pot might have some interesting exchanges.
Lucy (oldest known human/primate ancestor) Obviously she wouldn't be the greatest conversationalist but it would be fascinating to see an ancestor who's twelve million years old.
Napoleon I'd just be interested to see what he's like.
Bill Clinton I'd like him to speak with the other guests and learn from them, and I'd like to figure out what he's genuinely concerned about.
Albert Einstein Smart guy. Might have some good questions and comments, and probably knows some good jokes, too.

Slobodan Milosevic See Hitler and Pol Pot, and, in his case, I'd be curious to see what Christ and he would have to say to one another, seeing as Milosevic is ostensibly a Christian.
My mother She died recently and I miss her. I'd like to see her and ask her what things are like after death.

location The lodge where they filmed *The Shining*.

menu Catering by a variety of New York's nice vegetarian restaurants.
Cash bar (we don't want people getting too drunk.)

music Nice and unobtrusive classical music: Bach, Rodrigo, Satie etc.

toast It's been an interesting thousand years, filled with lots of good and, obviously, with lots of bad. Perhaps in the next thousand years we can stop intentionally hurting each other and learn how to be humble, forgiving and non-judgmental, and ultimately accepting of one another even when we completely disagree. The greatest enemies that we seem to face as human beings are arrogance and tribalism. When we can overcome these two things we will genuinely have accomplished something.

cash bar... we don't want people getting too drunk

Vincent Van Gogh

Buddha

Napoleon

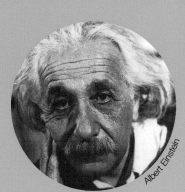

Albert Einstein

I'm a novelist and screenwriter; I've written thirteen novels and several TV dramas.

Deborah Moggach

everything matters but nothing matters that much...

guests William Brown Because I've always loved the 'William' books and he is my favourite person in the world.
Oscar Wilde Because he would make me wittier too.
Charles Dickens He would relish a huge dinner party and he might do some theatricals.
Darcey Bussell [*host*] She would be an adornment to any gathering, and she could dance for us.
Jessye Norman And she could sing for us...
Andras Schiff...while he plays the piano.
David Niven Because he was supposed to be such a charmer.
Peter Ustinov For his stories...
Judith Leyster She could tell us about being a woman and a painter in 17th-century Holland.
Elizabeth Bennet She could tell us about being a Jane Austen heroine.
George Gershwin He could play for us too...

Darcey Bussel

Charles Dickens

location On a remote beach in Goa.

menu Huge mounds of barbecued seafood, piles of fresh fruit (mangoes, strawberries, papaya), hot crusty bread, big pieces of Parmesan cheese, old Claret, and 'poire William' bitter chocolates.

seating plan Myself, William Brown, Darcey Bussell (William is susceptible to beautiful women), David Niven (who would charm her), Charles Dickens, Jessye Norman and Andras Schiff (for their duets), Judith Leyster and Elizabeth Bennet (so they can exchange notes), Oscar Wilde, George Gershwin (so he can play next to me).

music Bach cello suites, because they would be soothing and spiritual and would make us pause to think.

toast Everything matters but nothing matters that much...

Oscar Wilde... because he would make me wittier too

Oscar Wilde

Momo

Mourad Mazouz' London restaurant, Momo, specialises in traditional Moroccan and North African food with a modern style, and has been a huge success since it opened in 1997. 'I am like a volcano – sometimes quiet, sometimes explosive – generous, open... and doing things that make my life fun are real achievements for me.

guests Smaïl Mekki He is the funniest French comedian I know.
St Exupery He wrote and lived what I believe in the most.
Nushkat Fateh Ali Khan I love his music so much - it would bring great sound.
Pamberi Steel Band A group of Trinidadian musicians who laugh and dance while performing.
Claude Challe For me, he is one of the original 'party animals'.
Madame Claude She had one of the best 'call girl' companies ever.
Marc, the chef from Nobu He is a very 'naughty' man and makes great food.
Miss Piggy I could watch her all night.
Roberto Benigni Because life is beautiful!
Rossi de Palma Not for her physical beauty.
Eve Only her, not Adam.
And 150 friends from all my travels.

location In India, in a small village called Kouri next to Jaisalmer, in the middle of the desert. I would put up a huge Indian tent.

seating plan Everybody on the floor around a big fire, with the musicians behind. No particular order so that everybody could sit together naturally.

music Music by the musicians who are also my guests, so it would be one big jam of music from the world.

toast Let us toast to love for each other; love for the earth, which really needs it; love for the differences that exist on this planet. Let us follow the love that exists in our hearts.

Roberto Benigni

Miss Piggy

recipes

Mechouia
(Stewed peppers with tomatoes)

1kg / 2 lb 4 oz tomatoes, skinned, halved and de-seeded
75g / 2 ¾ oz peppers, halved and de-seeded
2 garlic cloves, crushed
4 tablespoons chopped fresh coriander
A teaspoon ground cumin
Half a teaspoon paprika
3 tablespoons olive oil
Salt and pepper

Grill the tomatoes and peppers until the pepper skins are black and blistering. Put the peppers in a bowl, cover with cling film and leave till cool enough to handle. Then remove the skins. Crush the tomatoes. Heat the oil in a saucepan, add the tomatoes and leave to cook to a purée.
Cut the pepper flesh into small pieces and add to the purée. Mix in well and add the garlic, coriander and spices. Leave to cook for 20 minutes, stirring from time to time.
Serve cold.

Lamb and prune tagine

(Serves 3-4)

600g / 1 lb 5 oz prunes
500ml / 18 fl oz water
100g / 3 ½ oz butter
1 kg / 2 ¼ lb lamb, cut in chunks
1 teaspoon ground cinnamon
2 cinnamon sticks
300g / 10 ½ oz sugar
100ml / 3 ½ fl oz orange-blossom water
2 apples
Salt and pepper

Bring the water to the boil and add the prunes. Remove from the heat and leave for 30 minutes, so the prunes absorb most of the water and swell up. Melt the butter in a tagine dish or flameproof casserole dish, add the meat and let it cook gently. Sprinkle on the ground cinnamon and add the cinnamon sticks. Add the sugar, little by little. Then add the orange-blossom water and pour in enough water to cover. Bring to the boil and then simmer for 20 minutes. Add the drained prunes. Peel, core and thinly slice the apples and add them to the dish. Cook for another 20 minutes. Check the seasoning and serve.

Pastilla de dattes
(Paper-thin pastries, filled with dates)

150g / 5 ½ oz dried dates
Lemon juice
3 drops almonds essence
Ground cinnamon
1 tablespoon orange-blossom water
1 tablespoon sugar
As many sheets of breikh (or filo) pastry as you want pastilla
Oil, for deep-frying

Take out the pips from the dates and mash them to a paste with the lemon juice, almond essence, ground cinnamon, orange-blossom water and sugar.
Lay out the pastry sheets and put a spoonful of filling in the middle of each. Roll up the pastry to enclose the filling, tucking in the edges neatly. Heat the oil for deep-frying until a cube of day-old bread browns in about a minute. Deep-fry the pastilla until golden and crisp. Drain on kitchen paper and keep warm while you cook the rest. Serve at once.

Chris Moon

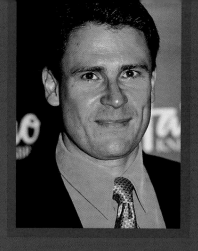

Former Army officer who worked for the charity, HALO, clearing anti-personnel mines. 1993 survived Khmer Rouge kidnap. 1995 lost lower right arm and leg in mine blast. 1996 completed London Marathon to help amputees in Cambodia. 1997 Great Sahara Run. Now ultra-marathoner, charity supporter, and author of *One Step Beyond*.

guests **Jesus** It is his 2000th, so it would be rude not to invite him.
Adolf Hitler I want to see his face when he realises who's sitting either side of him.
Albert Einstein I admire and want to meet anyone who is good at physics.
Lenny Henry Because I like him and he is funny.
William Wilberforce I admire the man who campaigned his entire life to ban slavery.
Margaret Thatcher [*host*] To act as MC (someone has to be in charge).
Nelson Mandela Hopefully the other guests will learn something from him.
Kate Adie (in flying suit) To report on the proceedings.
Saint Francis of Assisi Representing the poor, and environmental issues.
Lt. Col. Colin Mitchell (founder of the HALO trust) A good soldier, officer and friend. It would be good to see him again and he'd be very good at keeping unruly guests in order.
Slobodan Milosevic He's got some explaining to do.

location Angkor Wat Temple complex, Cambodia – because its not anyone's home territory and the history and current situation would promote interesting discussion.

music Copland: *Fanfare for the Common Man*.

toast Here's to the OLD, learning from humanity's mistakes and building a better future. Here's to the NEW, where the dignity of the individual is more important than a computer. A world where people go one step beyond ignorance and do their best. Where they control their instincts, learn forgiveness and stand the test.

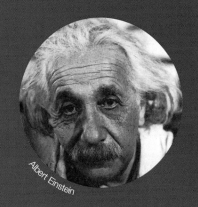
Albert Einstein

David Moorcroft

guests **John Walker** Led in a new generation of middle distance runners and was the inspiration for the Coe, Ovet and Cram era in the UK.
Peter Snell Great New Zealand athlete, three Olympic gold medals.
Murray Halberg Another great New Zealander - Olympic 5000m gold, 1960. Probably made more of his natural talent than any other runner of his time.
Cliff Temple Great friend, died in 1994, who loved distance running. Wonderful journalist and writer who would keep the conversation and laughter flowing.
Emil Zatopek Introduced huger work load, higher mileage and managed high risk approach to training.
Paave Nurmi Nine Olympic gold medals. 'greatest of the great' finish runners who revolutionised endurance events in the 1920s and 1930s.
Chris Chataway [*host*] Like me, he had one great moment as 5000-metre World Record holder, beating Vladimir Kuts in London in 1954.
John Anderson My coach since I was fifteen. Inspirational figure and biggest influence on my life, he would relish discussing athletics with his fellow guests.
Tony Rogers Olympic 1500-metre finalist in

Former World 5000-metre record holder, 1978 and 1982. Commonwealth 1500 and 5000-metre champion. Now chief executive of UK Athletics.

Singer, lover, mother – all those things.

Morcheeba

1984, competing for New Zealand. Good friend who helped me a great deal. Could be a big influence on New Zealand runners of the future.

Kip Keino First of the great Kenyan athletes. Had a big impact on me in the 60s and 70s and was the inspiration for the emergence of central Africa as the greatest power in the history of running.

Steve Cram World record holder 1500 m and mile at European, Commonwealth and World championships. If he had the time, in between all his broadcasting commitments, he could have a massive influence on the future of British distance running.

location
The location would be on the beach at Memaunganui on the North Island of New Zealand. I have wonderful memories of walking, running and relaxing on the beach on hot, sunny, cloudless days.

toast
Thanks to everything that all my guests have done, not just to write the history of world endurance running, but to the inspiration they have given to generations of runners. The new Millennium will be every bit as exciting as the last for runners of all levels...thanks for the memories.

guests Friends and family first off.
Nina Simone I've haven't met her but I saw her recently – it was brilliant. I think she'd be a great laugh.
Bjork She's someone I really admire. It would be interesting to have a chat with her to see what's behind the public character.
Shirley Bassey Because I used to get called Shirley Bassey at school.
Wayne (from Flaming Lips) He looks like a quality character and I'd ask him to bring his little puppies along! (I saw him play at the Electric Ballroom and he'd brought his puppies).
Nick Cave Not met him...but for the wee hours of the morning.
Eddie Izzard Just recently got into him. I saw him on TV a while ago by myself and I was laughing aloud, which I think is a good indication.
Natalie Merchant I met her a couple of months ago and she was just really sweet.
Lou (from Lamb) I do like people from up north...and we could also talk about kids and touring and travelling.
Bob Marley Would be cool.
Nick Drake Really mellow acoustic singer for late night chilling.

location
At home. I'm moving down to Brighton into a converted fire station – all open plan, with nice squidgy carpets.

menu
Lots of sweets – Flying Saucers, Shrimps, Mojos, and all the old fashioned little sweeties. Plenty of red wine.

seating plan
Sitting on the big squidgy carpet...it's really, really squidgy! I've never trodden on anything like it...you'll have to take your shoes off!

toast
Because there's been a lot of talk about the world ending, a lot of people are asking, 'What would you do if the world ended tomorrow?', so my toast would be: 'Live like there's no tomorrow'.

Nina Simone

117

Piers Morgan

Editor of *The Mirror* newspaper: 'He was half as good as he thought he was.'

guests **Adam** To tell him to leave the apple next time. **Adolf Hitler** So I could punch him straight in the face. **Princess Diana** Because she was great fun and cheered up all our lives. **Dennis Bergkamp** The greatest footballer of all time. **Paul McCartney** So he could sing a few tunes over dinner. **Ben Bradley** Because whilst editor of *The Washington Post* he broke the Watergate investigation – the greatest scoop of them all. (But he can only come if he tells me the identity of Deep Throat.) **Sir Donald Bradman** The greatest sportsman of all time. **William Shakespeare** So I can teach him how to spell. **Winston Churchill** Because he is what Britain should be all about. **My wife, Marion** Because she would be furious if I didn't invite her. **My mother** Because she would be more upset.

location Arsenal Stadium – Highbury.

menu A six-course feast prepared by Marco Pierre-White, washed down with Château Latour 61.

seating plan Hitler on his own. Everyone else can sit where they like.

music Wall to wall Beatles sung by Paul McCartney, with a guest appearance by Frank Sinatra; because you can't have a New Year's Eve party without *New York, New York* and *My Way*.

toast The toast would be an old saying of my grandmother's: 'Life ain't much but it's all you've got, so stick a geranium in your 'at and be 'appy!'

so I can teach him how to spell   William Shakespeare

Sheridan Morley

Sheridan Morley is a broadcaster, journalist and biographer. He is the drama critic of *The Spectator* and *The International Herald Tribune*. He presents the Radio 2 Arts program every Saturday evening and has written biographies of such stage and screen luminaries as David Niven and Audrey Hepburn: 'I have never been able to work a toaster.'

Desmond Morris

Desmond Morris is a well known author, broadcaster and zoologist. His pioneering work on human behaviour was first brought to the public's notice in 1967 with the publication of *The Naked Ape*. As a painter he has contributed significantly to the Surrealist movement in Britain.

guests I am allowed 11 guests. This number implies a 'last supper' scenario, so I have limited myself to male guests. I have only selected those who I have known personally; in this way I can be certain that they will be good company. The problem with choosing some great name from the past is that, in person, they might turn out to be a 'dinner bore'. So I am only selecting people who have proved to be fascinating company...

David Attenborough Naturalist.
Francis Bacon Artist.
Marlon Brando Actor.
Gerald Durrell Naturalist.
Barry Humphries [*host*] Humourist.
Stanley Kubrick Director.
Konrad Lorenz Zoologist.
John Lennon Musician.
Louis Malle Director.
Spike Milligan Humourist.
Dylan Thomas Poet.

location Assuming the party has to take place on 31st December / 1st January, I would have a huge 'big top' tent thrown over Stonehenge.

menu Medieval ox-roast, plenty of ice-cream, plenty of booze.

toast No toasts permitted.
Toasts on special occasions are full of pompous, pious clichés. They interfere with good conversation and should be outlawed.

I have never been able to work a toaster

guests My entire family, including all ex-husbands and wives, going back at least four generations and forward at least three.

location On a beach in Hawaii.

Blake Morrison

Blake Morrison is a poet, librettist, novelist, journalist and children's author

guests

Socrates For wisdom.
Helen of Troy For beauty.
Dr. Johnson For wit.
Aphra Benn For adventure.
Leonardo da Vinci Renaissance man.
Queen Hatshepsut For gender-bending.
Oskar Schindler For beating the system.
Desdemona For guilessness.
Holden Caulfield For un-phoniness.
Lucky Jim For irreverence.
Willy Wonka For entrepreneurialism.

location Key West or Sanibel Island, Florida.

toast Goodbye to all the bad bits: war, plague, famine, injustice, snobbery, prejudice, ignorance, and God. Hello again to the good, and let us see more of them: love, health, longevity, intelligence, art, democracy, equality, justice and technological advancement. Immortality? Time travel? A climate which humans can control? We who are living now will not see them, but all are possible – you, the future, will have to decide.

Socrates

Andrew Morton

Andrew Morton is the author of the controversial biographies *Diana - Her True Story,* and *Monica's Story*.

Racing driver

Stirling Moss

guests My father I would really like him to see how my later life turned out.

Juan Manuel Fangio An influence in my life almost as profound as that of my father's.

Ascari As a young driver, there were so many questions I wanted to ask him.

David Haynes My closest friend. Having shared every important occasion in my life for the last fifty-plus years, I can't imagine this particular party without him.

Winston Churchill Who would turn down the opportunity of having him at your dinner party?

Joan of Arc Reckon she must be a truly fascinating lady. Like Ascari, there are many questions I would like to put to her.

Peter Ustinov [*host*] He could keep me and all my guests wonderfully amused, added to which, he is quite capable of being anyone I forgot to invite!

Mary Tyler Moore To add glamour and sparkle to the occasion.

My wife So she can remind me what questions I wanted to put to my fascinating guests. With me, that would make ten; I wouldn't invite anyone else because ten is the maximum I enjoy at the dinner table.

Location Seabourne ship (any of the three) at sea in a non-humid area.

music If anything, very soft background stuff only. As the average age of the guests is rather high and our levels of hearing probably rather low, anything louder would mean none of us could enjoy the conversation!

toast Values to return...and patriotism.

Juan Manuel Fangio

Peter Ustinov

guests
Don Revie
Freddie Trueman
Michael Parkinson [*host*]
Geoffrey Boycott
Harold Wilson
J. B. Priestley
Dickie Bird
Alan Bennett
Keith Waterhouse
Russell Harty
James Mason
Charles Lawton

location Ilkley Moor.

menu Yorkshire pudding and wild grouse. Tetley's Yorkshire Bitter.

music Brighouse and Rastrick Brass band.

toast It wasn't like this in our day.

Michael Parkinson

James Mason

Andrew Motion

Poet Laureate.

guests **Bob Dylan** Genius.
Alfred Tennyson Genius.
John Keats Genius and liberal hero.
Oliver Cromwell Honourable.
Geoffrey Chaucer Genius.
Elizabeth Bishop Genius.
Cleopatra Need I say?
Emily Dickinson Genius.
Boadicea Honourable.
Elizabeth I Genius.
Shakespeare He would enjoy
meeting Cleopatra.
My wife Of course.

location My house - it's quiet, and
the children would like to meet the guests.

menu Asparagus from my garden; sea bass
caught by me; chocolate something;
lots of drink.

Mo Mowlam

To history, it's great, don't forget it, but don't live in it

Marjorie Mowlam has been the
Secretary of State for Northern
Ireland since 3rd May, 1997.

Mr Blobby

Misunderstood

guests

Richard III ...'cos he was misunderstood as well.

Buster Keaton My hero.

Houdini My hero, plus he'd be good for the cabaret.

Billy Connolly The funniest man alive.

Bagpuss My mate.

Mo Mowlam [host] She cheekily pinched my bum on *Live and Kicking*. A modern day heroine.

A wise aborigine ...'cos there's more to life than we know.

My family To whom I owe so much and without whom etc. etc.

Noel Edmonds Also without whom.....

William Shakespeare... at Bagpuss's request.

Editor of Hello magazine (Maggi Koumi) To pay for the whole darn thing.

location
A beach in Mauritius. That way the other 435 people I should have invited won't find us.

seating plan
Please mill at will – not Will Shakespeare.

music
The Steps, to catch the nuances in their music.

toast
Here's to life. (There, that should cover everything.)

Billy Connolly

Buster Keaton

> Mo Mowlam... she cheekily pinched my bum on 'Live and Kicking'... a modern day heroine

guests
Napoleon
Gandhi
Catherine the Great
Peter Cook
Noel Coward
Stalin
Bessie Smith
Billie Holiday
Jimi Hendrix
Tom Lehrer
Jack Nicholson

location
The Pavilion, Brighton.

menu
Fish and chips.
Vodka Red Bull and vodka Martini.

music
Compilation of 60s rock, Fats Waller, and Tom Lehrer, building to a crescendo with Noel Coward's *Mad Dogs and Englishmen*.

toast
To history - it's great, don't forget it, but don't live in it. Tomorrow - let's live in peace and respect each other. Enjoy and have fun.

Jimi Hendrix

John Julius Norwich

An ageing popular historian (the adjective referring to the intellectual level of my writing rather than the sales figures), with a weakness for lecturing and playing night-club piano, preferably in Venice.

guests

Benjamin Disraeli
Mrs. Patrick Campbell
S.T.Coleridge (when young)
Tallulah Bankhead
Noel Coward
Dorothy Parker
George Eliot
Isaiah Berlin
Martha Gellhorn
Oscar Wilde
Nancy Mitford
All chosen for the quality of their conversation.

location
The Grand Véfour in Paris; for beauty and atmosphere and general elitism.

menu
Beluga caviar with vodka
Filets de sole bonne femme with Gewürztraminer
Steak au poivre with Château Latour 1978
Mixed sorbets with Beaume de Venise

seating plan
I should mix them up around the main course but in a circle, as follows: Disraeli, Nancy Mitford, Oscar Wilde, Martha Gellhorn, Isaiah Berlin, George Eliot, myself, Dorothy Parker, Noel Coward, Tallulah, Coleridge, Mrs. Patrick Campbell.

toast
No toast, since the Millennium won't begin for another year. Besides, with talkers like these, who needs speeches?

music
None; it would ruin the conversation.

Dorothy Parker

Benjamin Disraeli

Leading international photographer. Terry O'Neill has photographed the Queen, Frank Sinatra, John F. Kennedy, and almost every leading politician, musical and film star of the past 40 years.

Terry O'Neill

seating plan

L.Marvin
C.Grant
S.Davis
A.Pacino
T.O'Neill
J.Kennedy
Sinatra
De Niro
B.Lancaster
P.Newman
W.Beatty
D.Martin

guests

I have worked and spent some time with these people over the last forty years. They are simply the best. It's the ultimate 'boys night out'.

Frank Sinatra
John Kennedy
Dean Martin
Warren Beatty
Cary Grant
Burt Lancaster
Robert de Niro
Al Pacino
Paul Newman
Lee Marvin
Sammy Davis Jnr.

I have worked and spent some time with these people... they are simply the best. It's the ultimate 'boys night out'

location

Harry's Bar, South Audeley St, W1 – best restaurant in the world, run by the inimitable Mark Bisley.

menu

Recommended by maître d' Mario at Harry's Bar:
Filetto di pollo e astice in gelatina d'astice
Pappa al pomodoro e mazzancolle
Bucatini all'astice vivo
Grigliata di crostacci, olio pesto crudo
Souffle alle ciliege e Kirsch, ragu di ciliege
White wine: Dreams - Jermann
Red wine: Borgogno - Riserva
Dessert wine - Acininobili

music

I would hire a band: Gene Harris - piano; Ray Brown - bass; Jeff Hamilton - drums; Stan Getz and Zoot Zims - tenor sax's. And let Frank, Dean and Sammy have a ball!

toast

One Millennium down, one more to go.

Paul Newman

Cary Grant

125

Jason Orange

Jason Orange was a member of the band Take That. Since they broke up in 1996, he has pursued an acting career. He was recently seen in the Channel 4 drama *Killer Net* and in a play called *GOB* at the King's Head Theatre in London.

Kylie Minogue

Let the next Millennium be not about breast jobs, mobile phones and Liz Hurley's new dress

guests Bradley Lincoln (best friend). He's my soul brother, a beautiful, loyal friend who would be there with full support to make sure the party is a success.
Max Beesley (best friend). Good energy. Life and soul of the party. Does good impressions and tells funny jokes, (can't dance though).
Simon Orange, Justin Orange, Dominic Orange (Three of five brothers)
Madeline Floyd An elegant, classy woman. Her artwork will soon be well known.
Neil Young Godfather of grunge, rock and roll hippy, mellow master of previous life times. He'd be there by the fire at the philosophical end.

Emily (fictional character). A ballet dancer with a Scorpio sign. She would have a heavenly body and hypnotic moon eyes.
Gio Kinkladze (footballer). When it gets to that stage of the evening when the boys want to start impressing the women, Gio can put us all back in our place by displaying his football skills (poetry in motion). I'd be his partner in the Wembly doubles.
Kahil Gibran He's a poet, a painter, a philosopher, and author of *The Prophet*, my favourite book.
Buxom Blonde You know the type, chatty, flirtatious...
Kylie Minogue One in every two men, I'm

sure, fancies her. Besides, she's friendly and up for a laugh.

music *Great gig in the sky, Time*, and *Comfortably Numb* – Pink Floyd.

toast

It is our job... in the next Millennium, to sort out the bollocks. Let us rid ourselves of the desire for instant gain and gratification. Let the next Millennium be not about breast jobs, mobile phones and Liz Hurley's new dress.
Let it be about fun and love and happiness in each others fragile and short lives.

Ozzy Osbourne

The Clivedon in Maidenhead

Jimmy Stewart I loved all of his movies. I could watch them again and again.
Randy Rhoads My one true friend, who I will always miss.
John Thomas Osbourne (my dad) I would like to have my dad see me now – to see what I've become – as he didn't have the opportunity before he died.

location Clivedon in Maidenhead, England. An historic and stately home in the English countryside, now owned by Bill Gates.

menu Cream of tomato soup. Traditional English Sunday dinner: turkey, mashed potatoes, gravy, stuffing, petit pois, Yorkshire pudding and trifle for dessert. No alcohol, as I don't drink.

music My guest, Elton John, would provide the soundtrack for the party.

toast Well, since Martin Luther King was one of the greatest speakers ever to have lived, I think I would let him do the toast.

guests

Winston Churchill No doubt he'll have some good war stories to tell.
Princess Diana I saw her grow up in the press over the years, from a child bride to a mother. I think she was one of the most beautiful women in the world. I will always believe that her death was no accident.
Marilyn Monroe The sexiest woman who ever lived. She had timeless beauty and I would love her to sing Auld Lang Syne at midnight.

Elton John He's a friend and a real character. He would be the ultimate entertainment for the evening.
John Lennon My idol, my hero…a legend. He's the reason why I'm in the music business.
Oprah Winfrey She has an amazingly warm personality and great intelligence.
Martin Luther King He was a true humanitarian. A saint.
Bob Hope One of the funniest men who ever lived. I always had great respect and admiration for him.

127

Gary Pallister

Gary Pallister plays for Middlesbrough Football Club. Position: defender. Capped 22 times for England.

Sean Connery

guests Adolf Hitler To try and see what made him tick, the cause of the hatred.
Oskar Schindler To watch him and Adolf talk through a few things.
Winston Churchill …to sit next to Hitler.
Cameron Diaz She would brighten the place up a bit.

Mary, my girlfriend
Elvis Less for the music than to find out about how he died.
Jack Nicholson He knows how to enjoy himself.
James Bond (Sean Connery) For a bit of sophistication.
Billy Connolly He's dead funny and would be great for the after-dinner entertainment.

Marilyn Monroe Ditto above, but also to find out more about how she died.
Jesus …well, you'd have to.

seating plan
Churchill and Schindler next to Hitler, everyone else where they want.

Michael Parkinson

Michael Parkinson has been interviewing celebrities on his BBC chat show for many years.

toast 'We've come a very long way in the last Millennium to care for the world's children. Let's make them our first priority in the next.'

128

Matthew Parris

Former politician turned journalist, writer and broadcaster. Best known in *The Times*.

Jane Austen

James Cook

Henry, VII... he'd be no fun at all but I'd like to shake his hand.

guests

Noel Coward Wit, style and mischief.

David Hume (rationalist, 18th century Scottish historian / philosopher) Honesty, originality and dry humour.

The Baroness Trumpington (Tory whip in the Lords) Kind, funny, brazen – a wonderful, 40 Capston-a-day, dry, deep voice. Plus anecdotes.

Cole Porter Sophisticated, cynical, sentimental and wise.

Captain James Cook To tell me of his adventures.

Jane Austen Catty, perceptive, good-hearted, observant.

John Major For courtesy, good nature and charm.

Elizabeth I I admire her but consider her a mystery; I want to know her better.

Rodney (*Only Fools and Horses*) Don't-cha just love him!

My mum She'll soon get everyone related and laughing.

Henry VII My hero. He'd be no fun at all but I'd like to shake his hand.

location Machu-Picchu, Peru – mystery, human achievement, natural beauty.

menu Simple, so as not to intrude on the conversation. Bread, soup, beef and potatoes, bread and butter pudding. Beer, cider and water. Fruit to follow, especially mangoes.

music Country and Western.

toast To the twilight of the gods – and the dawn of reason.

Tony Parsons

Tony Parsons is a broadcaster, journalist, and novelist.

guests

Frank Sinatra The greatest singer.
Cyd Charisse The greatest dancer.
Muhammad Ali The greatest fighter.
Stephen Hawking The greatest thinker.
Brigitte Bardot The greatest beauty.
Ernest Hemingway The greatest writer.
Naomi Campbell The greatest legs.
Pablo Picasso The greatest painter.
Elizabeth Taylor The greatest eyes.
John Lennon The greatest Beatle.
Susan George The greatest mouth.

location   Victoria Peak, Hong Kong.

menu   Dan-dan noodles, bang-bang chicken, sweet and sour soup, Bejing duck and a crate of Bolinger - simple, but celebratory.

music   Sinatra and Lennon will sing and Cyd Charisse and I will dance.

seating plan

Cyd Charisse	Stephen Hawking
Brigitte Bardot	John Lennon
Tony Parsons	Naomi Campbell
Muhammad Ali	Pablo Picasso
Frank Sinatra	Elizabeth Taylor
Susan George	Ernest Hemingway

It's a conventional boy/girl seating plan, with an attempt to keep Sinatra, Hemingway and John Lennon apart - we don't want a fight.

toast   To the glory of mankind, and to the fact that the century that produced mass murderers and their willing henchmen also produced the great and the glorious figures at this table.

Tony Parsons' latest book, *Man and Boy* is published by Harper Collins.

Pablo Picasso

Liz Taylor

Frank Sinatra

John Lennon

Brian Patten

Brian Patten has been instrumental in the renaissance of poetry and public performance in Britain for both children and adults.

The child's imaginative world is without Time
The Secret garden will never age;
The tangled undergrowth remains as fresh
As when the author put down her pen.
Its mysteries are as poignant now as then.

Though Time's a thief it cannot thieve
One page from the world of make believe.

On the track the Railway Children wait;
Alice still goes back and forth through the glass;
In Tom's Midnight Garden time unfurls,
And children still discover secret worlds.

At the Gates of Dawn Pan plays his pipes;
Mole and Ratty still float in awe down-stream.
The weasels watch, hidden in the grass.
None cares how quickly human years can pass.

Though Time's a thief it cannot thieve
One page from the world of make believe.

Andi Peters

Blimey me, I'm just me, doing what I do.

guests Jill Dando Jill loved a good fun evening, and she was always great company. Emma Forbes [*host*] My best friend and a fine cook, so there would be no burnt food. Gary Barlow He would play the piano, and help with all the sing-alongs. Nelson Mandela I'd just love to meet him. Ruggie One of my best friends, so he'd have to come. Mum, Dad, two brothers, sister My family are very important to me, so they'll all have to come along. Brandon Starkie He's a mad friend who'll keep everyone amused.

location It would be held on a hot sunny day, outside, in massive grounds. Australia would be nice, but I really don't mind.

menu Lots of seafood, and Thai food which is a fave of mine. There'd be loads of Ribena, and good beer and wine.

music The new Spice Girls album

toast I'm a man of few words... "Marvellous, it's a new year."

Nelson Mandela

Popeye

guests Ahoy, mates! Me fantasky feast 2000 wouldst have to includes all me frien's, 'cause they've shared the good times and the bad wi' me in THIS millennium.

Olive Oyl 'Cause from the firs' time she kissed me, she's been me sweet patootie, my only goil!

Swee' Pea 'Cause he's me adoptid kid, my li'l Swee' Pea.

J.Wellington Wimpy 'Cause Wimpy's got 24 college degrees, a lofty IQ, and even tho' he drives me nuts, he's me frien'. Frien's is the mos' importink thing on eart', even if ya can't stan' 'em!

Elzie Segar The worl's greatest cartoonist, 'cause in his Thimble Theater comic strip, me 1929 cameo turned into a permanent role, and, ever since, I yam what I yam - a sailor man star.

Noah 'Cause he built a magnifiskent invention; his ark was the poifeckt home for all the pairs of creatures, when the big flood came. Besides, when all the rain stopped, he still had a terrificks way to go sailin', sailin' over the bounding main !

Christopher Columbus 'Cause he set sail across the ocean blue in fourteen hun'nert 'n' ninety two, with nots one, but three ships, and finds a whole new conktinent. Not bad for a swab wi'out a compass!

Vasco de Balboa A swab who kept sailin' the ocean so far, he founds a whole 'nother ocean - the Pacific!

Neil Armstrong A lucky swab, to be able to sails all the way to the moon! And when he gots there, he was the first to take one small step for man, one giant step for mankind. By the way, didja know tha' asides from lots of green cheese and moon rocks, there's a Sea of Tranquillity up there? Terrificks port o' call for a sailor man to visit!

Brutus Well, blow me down! It's a new Millennium, an' even me ol' enemy should joins in the fun!

The inventor of the punching bag A great li'l gadget so I can stays in ship-shape - just in case I changes me mind about invitin' Brutus.

The inventor of canned spinach A true geniusk. Besides, I'll tell 'em all it's a BYOS (bring your own spinach) party. Ya can never haves enough spinach!

location Aboard The Olive, me ship, 'cause it's stocked ta the gills with SPINACH!

menu Canned spinach, fresh spinach, spinach salad, spinach soup, creamed spinach, spinach quiche, spinach tacos, spinach pie, and maybe a ton o' hamburgers for me frien', Wimpy. (And he won't have to pay me till Tuesday!), sauteed spinach, spinach souffle, spinach pasta, pickled spinach...

music Me favourite song, *I'm Popeye the Sailor Man*, and a bunch of sea chanteys.

toast Let's hope tha' in the new Millennium everybody can live peacefully and harmoniously together. And if ya has any enemies, jus' let me know. Me famous twister sock'll takes care of 'em.

Gail Porter

Children's television programme presenter, Gail Porter has worked on both ITV and BBC.

guests
Frank Sinatra
Judy Garland
Liza Minnelli
Ewan McGregor
Pee Wee Herman
Robbie Williams
Manic Street Preachers
Suggs
Space
Eddie Izzard
My mum, brother, grandpa, gran
Ali G
Frank Skinner
Dawn French
Jennifer Saunders
Joanna Lumley
Steve Tyler
Vinny Jones
Chris Evans
Pete and Geoff and Charlotte
and me mates!

Robbie Williams

location Blackpool Pleasure Beach.

menu Oysters, strawberries and champagne. (Chips for my mum!!)

music 80s classics!!

toast Everyday is a gift and life is sweet...let's make it sweeter!!

Eddie Izzard

Ken Pyne

"ELIZABETH TAYLOR COULDN'T COME -"HER BACK'S PLAYING UP AGAIN"

CELEBRITY MILLENNIUM PARTY!

Jonathan Pugh

I have been the front-page pocket cartoonist for *The Times* since January 1996. My work has also appeared in *The Independent*, *The Guardian*, *The Observer*, *Private Eye*, *The Spectator* and *The New Statesman*.

seating plan

Henri Cartier-Brsson Vermeer Cleopatra myself Sempe George Cruickshank Spock John Updike Stephan Fry Anna Pugh Mervyn Pugh Martha Gellhorn

guests

Anna Pugh, my wife

Vermeer I have never seen an artist who paints so beautifully; there are so many questions I would like to ask him.

Jean Jacques Sempe My favourite living cartoonist and an enormous influence; it would be wonderful to meet him.

Mervyn Pippin Pugh, My grandfather who died in 1962, the year before I was born; by all accounts, a remarkable man.

Martha Gellhorn I don't know of a more courageous or inspirational journalist; her stories would be rivetting.

George Cruickshank (1792–1878) An inspirational cartoonist; I would like him to sketch the evening, leaving me with the most wonderful memento.

Cleopatra To find out if she really was as sexy and smart as history tells us.

Stephen Fry I find him extremely funny. A wonderful raconteur and a great leveller who I am sure would amuse all.

Henri Cartier–Bresson The most glorious photographer; I'd like him to photograph the evening and send me the originals.

Spock (*Star Trek*) Hopefully he would give me a few answers to the mysteries of the universe.

John Updike I can't think of any living novelist I would rather meet. (He also happens to draw cartoons.)

location A candle-lit table in the main square in Vicenza, Italy. I fell in love with the city when I went there on my honeymoon.

menu Fish soup followed by roast lamb, gratin dauphinois, flageolet beans, and roasted garlic. Cheese followed by fresh fruit.
Champagne, Clos de Mesnil, Krug, Puligny Montrachet (1971), and Petrus (1947). Pudding wine: Château d'Yquem (1962).

music Schubert's complete Impromptus (piano), followed by Nina Simone, then Van Morrison.
I would christen the new Millennium with Lois Armstrong's *What a Wonderful World*.

toast A toast to more laughter in the new Millennium and less bloodshed.

Suzy Quatro

Most famous as an entertainer with 16 hit records, Suzy also played the part of Leather Toscadero in *Happy Days*, and appeared in *Minder, Dempsey and Makepiece, Annie Get Your Gun* and *Tallulah Who?*. She has her own talk radio show on Radio 2.

guests

Beethoven A fascinating manic depressive. My favourite composer and I would love to talk with him; not that he would hear me! And to have him play. Wonderful - the Abba of the classical world!

Richard Gere For the after dinner celebration - one to one - know what I mean?

Marilyn Monroe If I'm going to be upstaged by anyone, it would have to be her - the most gorgeous, sexy, innocent, underrated, intelligent human being ever.

Elvis Presley Because I missed the chance to meet him at Graceland and have regretted it ever since.

My mother My inspiration throughout my life. Wish I could have one more conversation with her, and this would be the perfect opportunity.

Laura My 17 year old daughter - just because I love her and value her friendship and company.

Richard My 15 year old son because he's 6'2" tall, he's so outspoken, he makes me laugh, and because he's mine.

Rainer My husband, to take that one glass of champagne I don't need, out of my hands.

Tallulah Bankhead Ever since writing and starring in *Tallulah Who?*, I have been in love with this woman - outspoken, outrageous and in her own words, "pure as the driven slush" - my kind of woman.

Mother Teresa To keep a balance on the mayhem and to remind everyone how unselfish some people can be.

J.F. Kennedy Necessary when the subject of conversation leaves religion and veers over to politics. Every good dinner party needs a heated debate... and to keep Miss Monroe company, of course.

location

My dining room, in my 15th century Elizabethan manor house, finished in 1590. So much history must add to the ambiance of the event.

seating plan

Me on one end, Richard Gere to my left to enable me to play footsie, unseen by my husband who would be seated at the other end, and nowhere near Marilyn - cruel but fair.

Next to Richard would be Mother Teresa - ha ha ha!

Next to mother Teresa would be Marilyn Monroe, and in direct contact across from her would be J.F.Kennedy - we could all watch the sparks fly.

Elvis in between my husband and Tallulah. My husband is a big, big music fan and would eat this up, although he can't hold a tune in a bucket.

Next to my husband I would put Beethoven.

Next to Beethoven would be my daughter Laura who is well known for talking non-stop - I'm sure she would make Beethoven see his deafness in a different light.

Next to Laura, J.F. Kennedy, who I am sure would find her a delight. Next to J.F. Kennedy I would put my mother, who was very religious and I am sure would lecture Kennedy on his womanizing ways - better than telling dirty jokes, I think.

Then between my mother and me, my son Richard, who, besides always trying to run away from his grandma's hugs would also remind me what happens when you play footsie with someone like Richard Gere.

'I guess I am a person who loves to entertain and communicate. I plan to go on working until I can't – when I turn my back to the audience and shake my ass and there is no response, I will retire.'

Richard Gere

Elvis Presley

Marilyn Monroe

135

Gordon Ramsay

Footballer, turned cook, turned television star! Just kidding. I am just a cook striving for perfection and an elusive Michelin star!

guests

Pele My all-time hero.

Kenny Dalglish My second all-time hero.

Michelle Pfeiffer Miss Wet T-shirt 'par excellence'.

Meg Ryan Beauty, brains and a lot of fun.

Eric Clapton For those romantic moments...

Prince Naseem [*host*] Because you never know in life...

Baby Spice Peter Pan syndrome. Our 'inner child'?

Helena Christensen The perfect hostess.

Kate Moss Ditto above.

Phil Collins His music has been with me for so long that I need him alongside me to celebrate the new Millennium.

Tana, my wife She just has to be with me.

location

The isle of Pralin in the Seychelles. Not only one of the most beautiful places in the world, but one of the best diving sites as well (my favourite sport).

menu

Some recipes from my menu, of course: Oriental snapper salad, risotto with pan-roasted squid or marinated tuna with balsamic-dressed mooli, stir-fried monkfish with peppers and pak choi or a wonderful seafood paella.

White wines and a lot of 'bubbles' to wash it down with.

seating plan

I think Tana would love to sit in the middle between Phil and Eric. I am perfectly happy with Meg on one side, Baby Spice on the other, but with Pele not very far away!!

Rectangular table with Prince Naseem at top head of table and then moving clockwise as follows:

Kate Moss, Kenny Dalglish, Baby Spice, Myself, Meg Ryan, Pele (at opposite head), Michelle Pfeiffer, Eric Clapton, Tana, Phil Collins, Helena Christensen

music

Great music doesn't go off like fish! Let's have Eric and Phil with a little help from Baby Spice.

toast

Some wonderful things happened to me in the old Millennium. I was quite fond of him! But let's greet the new one. Let him surprise us with some new tricks and games and, personally, with that famous third star!!! May all your dreams come true.

Meg Ryan

Kate Moss

Seafood Paella

(serves 6-8)

A paella is a wonderful celebration of seafood, chicken, vegetables and rice all cooked together with paprika, garlic and, of course, saffron. It's important to have a good mix of seafood, although anything you can't find can be replaced with something similar, or left out altogether.

1.5 litres chicken stock
1 small to medium chicken, cooked
2 x 200g lobster tail, cooked
200g small squid, prepared
500g fresh mussels, de-bearded
1 x 200g monkfish tail, filleted
5 tbsp. olive oil
1 medium onion, finely chopped
1 medium leek, thinly sliced
½ small red pepper, chopped
½ small green pepper, chopped
6 ripe plum tomatoes, skinned, de-seeded and chopped
2 large cloves garlic, crushed
½ tsp. saffron strands
1 bay leaf
500g paella or Arborio rice
150ml dry white wine
200g raw langoustines or tiger prawns, peeled but last tail section left on
1 tsp. paprika
chopped fresh parsley to garnish
sea salt and freshly ground black pepper
Recommended wine: Spanish white Grenache

1. Prepare all the ingredients before you start cooking. Heat the chicken stock in a pan. Cut the cooked chicken into 8 joints using poultry shears or a heavy sharp knife. Discard the wing and leg tips and the back. Shell the lobster tails and cut the meat into chunks. Cut the squid tubes into rings, reserving the tentacles. Pick over the mussels and discard any that are open. Cut the monkfish fillets into chunks.
2. Heat half the oil in a paella pan or a large, shallow pan of 5-litre capacity. Sauté the onion, leek, peppers, tomatoes and garlic with the saffron and bay leaf for 5-10 minutes, or until the vegetables are softened. Stir in the rice and cook for 3-5 minutes, stirring until it turns opaque. Stir in the wine to de-glaze and cook until evaporated .
3. Ladle in the hot stock, allowing each amount to be absorbed before adding the next, and stirring very occasionally. Cooking should take about 15 minutes. When the rice has been cooking for about 10 minutes, add the mussels.
4. In the meantime, heat the remaining oil in a frying pan and sauté the monkfish chunks for about 3 minutes, stirring; remove. Add the squid rings and tentacles, the lobster pieces and langoustines or prawns. Stir until the langoustines or prawns just turn pink and feel firm. Take care not to overcook the seafood.
5. Stir all the cooked seafood and chicken pieces into the rice. Season with salt and pepper, then sprinkle over the paprika and mix in gently along with any remaining stock, (if the rice still seems a little chalky and undercooked, you can add some boiling water and cook for a further 6-8 minutes, or until everything is ready and the rice is plump.) Scatter over the parsley and serve accompanied by salad and crusty bread.

recipes

Stir-Fried Monkfish with Peppers and Pak Choi

(serves 4)

A very easy dish. Just spend a little time on the initial preparation and you'll find the cooking takes only minutes. You'll need a good sized, non-stick or well seasoned wok for this. Pak choi (also called bok choy) is a Chinese leafy vegetable, rather like Swiss chard. It is increasingly available in supermarkets but, if you can't find it, then use shredded Chinese leaves instead. Serve with a bowl of aromatic Thai jasmine rice sprinkled with a few toasted sesame seeds.

2 x 250g monkfish tails, filleted
2 tbsp. groundnut oil
1 small red pepper, thinly sliced
1 small yellow pepper, thinly sliced
1 small onion, thinly sliced
1 tbsp. chopped fresh ginger
1 medium courgette, sliced
100 g pak choi, coarsely shredded
50g fresh bean sprouts
2 tsp. light soy sauce
1 ½ tsp. Chilli Spice mix
2 tbsp. classic vinaigrette
1 tsp. sesame oil
sea salt and freshly ground black pepper

Alternative fish: peeled tiger prawns, about 400g

1. Remove any grey membrane from the monkfish, then cut across into 1cm slices. Make sure all the other ingredients are prepared before you start cooking.
2. Heat a large wok until almost smoking. Add 1 tablespoon of the oil and stir-fry the monkfish for about 3 minutes, until browned on both sides. Remove and drain on kitchen paper towels . Keep hot.
3. Add the remaining oil to the wok and heat well. Stir-fry the peppers, onion, ginger and courgette for about 2 minutes, until cooked and lightly coloured. Remove from the wok with a draining spoon and keep warm.
4. Reheat the oil and stir-fry the pak choi and bean sprouts for 2 minutes, or until just wilted. Mix in the soy sauce and 1 teaspoon of the spice mix. Mix the remaining 1/2 teaspoon of the spice mix into the vinaigrette. Set aside.
5. Return the other vegetables to the wok. Toss in the sesame oil and reheat until very hot. Check the seasoning. Divide among four warmed plates and arrange the monkfish on top. Trickle a little of the spicy vinaigrette on top of each portion, then serve.

Esther Rantzen

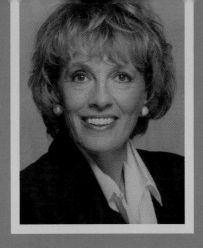

Esther Rantzen is a television presenter and producer. She campaigns against issues of child abuse and drug problems.

guests
Queen Elizabeth I
Shakespeare
Jane Austen
John Donne
Whoopi Goldberg
Billy Connolly
Charles Dickens
Dr. Johnson
Oscar Wilde
Desmond Wilcox
Eric Morecambe

I must apologise for the fact that there are not enough women guests - that's history for you!

location My Fantasy Feast would take place on a day in June in the Colombe d'Or restaurant in the beautiful medieval village of St Paul de Vence, in the south of France. We would have a long table under the vine-covered trellis next to the most spectacular view across the hills of Provence.

menu Caviar with hot toast. Wild salmon, cucumber salad. and new potatoes. Local French cheeses. Wild strawberries.

music Nina Simone, Mozart.

toast To love, laughter, tolerance and the pursuit of excellence - and the safety and happiness of children everywhere.

Nina Simone

Reef
Jack
Bessant

'I'm having a good go.'

guests Neil Armstrong Because he's been there.
Duke Kahanamoku Hawaiian surfing legend.
Catherine Zeta Jones 'Cause she owns a place in Malibu.
Mickey Dora Legendary party animal and surfer.

Helena Christensen Good style.
Jimi Hendrix and band For entertainment value.
James Sweet Always good conversation, and relaxed style for a party.

Raquel Welsh Circa *The Land that Time Forgot*.
Beth Orton 'Cause she's got soul.
Jools Holland Nickel bloke.
My brother Just to see him again.

location Margaret River, Australia.

menu The freshest seafood, beautiful Australian wine, champagne, water, tea, coffee.

toast To a new era!!

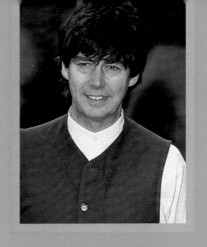

An award winning radio broadcaster, Mike Read has also written seven musicals, screenplays for three films, and hit songs for a diverse range of artists including Cliff Richard, King's College Choir, and His Majesty's Band in The Royal Marines. He is a tennis fanatic!

guests

Jesus With a caveat that we don't bombard him with too many questions. A conversational Jesus.

William Blake He would be there next to Jesus so they can discuss metaphysics and inspirations and things like that.

Hilaire Belloc Devout Catholic; a great walker; an anglophile; lived in Sussex; wrote a lot of inspirational things; and an MP. Like me he used to walk the South Downs a lot.

Rupert Brook For a variety of reasons. He was very inspired by Belloc and he invited Belloc up to King's when he was there. Also, I've written a biography, a film and stage musical about him and am Chairman of the New Rupert Brook Society and would like to know if he'd approve of all that - or if he'd say 'What have you done with my life, mate!'

Grace Kelly (seated next to Rupert Brook) It's a bit of matchmaking this one. She was probably one of the most beautiful women of the century - and she'd be seated next to Rupert Brook who, according to everyone, was one of the most beautiful men of the century. So we'd have two beautiful people with intelligence.

Sir John Betjeman (on Grace's other side.) Again, I've worked quite a bit of John Betjeman's work into my music, but I think he would be absolutely infatuated with Grace Kelly and would have been delighted to sit next to her.

Oscar Wilde (seated next to John Betjeman) They were both Magdalene men... same college... they would discuss poetry and he would be great for his sparkling conversation and wit.

Oliver Cromwell (seated next to Oscar) They would probably discuss their respective rises and falls together. They were both powerful and influential people with a whole string of acolytes and they both thought they were infallible.

Lady Jane Grey (next to Cromwell.) In her ten days as queen, she barely had time to have supper. She and Oliver could discuss the fact that they were two of the most peculiar leaders we've had this Millennium. (I'd sit next to her too).

C. B. Fry (on the other side of me.) He played cricket and football for England; was an athletic blue; probably our greatest all-rounder (he held the long-jump record for years). He was asked to captain England cricket XI at the age of 49. A bit of a womaniser too. Also, he was invited to be King of Albania at one point, so he could lean over me to discuss that matter with Lady Jane Grey. He would be opposite Hilaire Belloc so they wouldn't be able to talk too much. He was desperate to become an MP, and HB was one, so I thought they might irritate each other.

Richard Rodgers He doesn't do much speaking at the table, but he's going to be at the piano. He'll be doing some of his great classics like *Blue Moon* and *Manhattan* and *Some Enchanted Evening*. He's tinkering instead of talking; just background music.

Thomas Paine He'd be there - if I'm allowed an extra one - to discuss *The Rights of Man*.

location Al Fresco, on the South Downs, probably somewhere in West Sussex.

toast

I'd hope that Jesus would get up and come with a few well-chosen words.
Cromwell would make the toast, with his great one-liner: 'A few honest men are better than numbers'.

Oscar Wilde

Connor Reeves

London Soul singer, Connor Reeves has been described as the male Mariah Carey.

I am a chef and restaurateur who has dedicated the past 20 or more years of my life to the championing of British food. Through my

---

I would call my feast the *Meaning of Life Feast*, the purpose of which will be to gather together great examples of humanity from the last two millennia and discuss ways in which mankind could best evolve in the next.

guests **Yoda** To demonstrate 'the force', what it is, and how to access it.
Leonardo da Vinci To discuss human potential, motivation and the nature of genius.
Queen Elizabeth I To demonstrate how women can attain true equality in the still very patriarchal society of the third Millennium.
Freud & Jung As a pair – to debate the nature of man – sexual or spiritual.
Jesus To put people straight on what the bible really meant before it was edited, mistranslated and twisted to oppress the masses through fear.

Buddah To discuss with Jesus ideas of Karma, reincarnation and enlightenment.
Ramesses II To show how to become a living 'God-Man' in the new Millennium.
Eve To give her a chance to defend herself for being blamed for the fall of man.
Shakespeare To entertain with his latest works during courses.
Mr Creosote ...because it's the *Meaning of Life Feast* and if it's getting on a bit and you feel that 'the greatest examples of humanity' are getting on a bit, you can bring the meal to an end by offering Mr C a 'wafer thin mint', thus causing him to explode and encouraging the other guests to leave.

toast To Human Evolution.

guests **Martin Luther King** He gave me inspiration as a child. His voice keeps people spellbound.
Nelson Mandela One of the greatest figures of my time, if not the greatest.
Marilyn Monroe For me, she had the greatest figure.
Muhammad Ali Ali, at his peak, was a larger than life character; perfect for this larger than life table.
Princess Diana I miss her terribly.
Claude Monet I can't afford to own a Monet, but now at least I'd have him.
Enzo Ferrari I would have to see for myself the man who created the meanest machine.
Mrs. Beeton Having died so young, I thought she'd like to see the cooking of the Millennium.

Carl Jung

Sigmund Freud

Claude Monet

Gary Rhodes

Adam Rickitt

television series, cookery books and other products, I hope I have helped revive the British public's faith in their culinary traditions.

Stevie Wonder He's never out of tune with anything or anybody. 'Isn't he lovely?'
Kim Basinger She always makes me hungry.
Georgio Armani Neat, precise, clean and classic – sounds like my cooking.

location Seven-course meal with each course to be enjoyed at one of the seven wonders of the world. The finest places to see with the finest foods to eat.

music
Songs in the Key of Life - Stevie Wonder.
Millennium - Robbie Williams.

Adam Rickitt has recently left the television soap-opera *Coronation Street* to focus on his singing career. His first single, *I Breathe Again* went straight into the top ten: 'Determined, enthusiastic and loyal. Striving towards bettering a limited ability in the performing arts, inspired by others' examples and my own love for the job.'

guests Head of CIA So we could all chant 'We know something you don't know! Do da!'
Family and friends Welcoming a new era would be pointless without those who love you and whom you love.
J.F.K. To see if he knows who did it.
Gandhi To honour the bravest spiritual leader of the century.
Jennifer Lopez You did say *fantasy* feast.
James Bond He could act as security for the function and would be a great after–dinner speaker.

Bill Gates I'd make him serve us dinner!
Keith Richards In–house entertainment.
Billy Connolly To keep the atmosphere humorous.
Robbie Fowler
Alexander the Great A vital tactician to plan the evening's festivities.

location The Pyramids: a big club with laser shows coming off the pyramids and a dance floor in between.

menu Sushi and vodka and Red Bull (lots of ginger with the sushi.)

music Club music: Paul Oakenfold, Paul Van Dyk, Chemical Brothers, DJ Shadow

toast With the troubles of the past, we now look to the future, in the hope that man's wisdom will allow it the humility to change its ills, the strength to shepherd the weak, and the spirit to cherish the unloved. In the dawn of a new beginning we ask God for his guidance and leadership, that as one people we might follow the example of his devotion.

Kim Basinger

Jennifer Lopez

Bill Gates

141

Malcom Rifkind

Advocate, parliamentarian, minister. Now 'resting'.

guests **Leonardo da Vinci** Renaissance man, remarkable mind.

Napoleon Extraordinary achievements from humble beginnings. He could carve the roast.

Winston Churchill The greatest statesman of our history. He could make the main speech.

Elizabeth 1 A successful woman in a man's world.

Ghengis Khan Terrible, but would keep other guests in line.

Albert Einstein Would discover how we could pay for the meal.

Mary Queen of Scots Could compete with Elizabeth to decide on the menu.

Marlene Dietrich Superb and seductive singer, would entertain the guests.

Disraeli He said that whenever he wanted to read a good book, he wrote one!

Michelangelo Artist of genius. He could do the table decorations.

Moses Freedom fighter.

location

Edinburgh Castle; superb views.

menu Steak and chips, preceded by lobster and followed by wild strawberries.

seating plan In the order above with me in between Ghengis Khan and Churchill.

music Elgar

toast The future is not what it used to be.

Winston Churchill

Marlene Dietrich

Disraeli

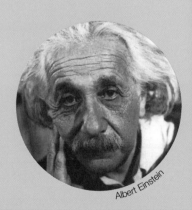

Albert Einstein

Riddell

Bruce Robinson

Screen writer and the writer of *Thomas Penman*.

guests **Bacchus** To keep his trap shut and bring the wine. (see menu)

Charles Dickens To heap praise on him and discuss the end of *Edwin Drood*.

Charles Baudelaire To kiss his cheek and tell him he was right (nearly).

J.Robert Oppenheimer To discuss certain secrets that he wouldn't believe, but that I would persuade him are true.

Margaret Thatcher So she couldn't get in! And yet I'd let her in, 'cos I'd like John Pilger to demolish her.

John Pilger Because I respect his passion more than any other journalist.

A substitute for myself Because I've been out the back with Bacchus and am too pissed to speak.

The entire Berlin Philharmonic Orchestra With 'you know who' conducting.

Edgar Allen Poe or someone similar Just love to hear him chant *The Raven*.

Kenneth Patchen, Mark Chagall, Bob Dylan, William Burroughs, John Bunyan, Henry Miller They'll have to sit on each other's laps!

Jack the Ripper To actually find out who he was.

location Anywhere but my house.

menu The best curry on earth and all the great Bordeaux; I won't be greedy and get into the 19th century, but Petrus, Chaval Black, Margaux, Béchevelle – years 1945, 1953, 1959, 1961 etc....

seating plan After the pre-dinner drinks, they won't need one. However, I want Charles Dickens within shouting distance.

music None, but maybe a saxophone somewhere.

toast Please God, let those not yet born not be messed-up by those long since dead. Please God, let not people choose the crap of our species to run our lives. Please God, let us be wise enough to dispense with politicians.

Margaret Thatcher

Bob Dylan

143

Gaby Roslin

Television presenter

guests Grace Kelly • Nelson Mandela • Madonna • Eric Morecambe • Princess of Wales • Woody Allen • Mo Mowlam • Albert Elnstein • Lily Savage • Jimmy Stewart • Lawrence Olivier

location On a private island in the Caribbean...dolphins would be swimming around...the party would start as the sun sets.

menu There would be a giant barbecue with endless tapas and grilled fish. Platters of exotic fruit for dessert with grilled bananas, sorbets and ice-cream. Champagne cocktails, frozen Margaritas and rum punch.

seating plan There would not be a seating plan; guests would come barefoot and probably end up sitting on the sand. It would be a very relaxed and comfortable atmosphere.

music Nothing slushy or slow. Something upbeat, as we'd all be looking excitedly into what the future might hold.

toast Thanks. You're welcome. (As in thanks to the old and welcome to the new.)

Thanks. You're welcome

Lily Savage

Woody Allen

Albert Roux

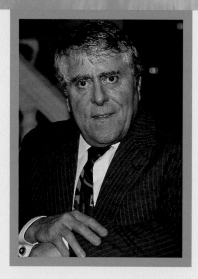

World renowned chef and creator of London's legendary Le Gavroche restaurant.

My fantasy feast to celebrate the incoming thousand years would be to sit with my granddaughter Emily, eating quail cooked sweet and sour in the Chinese style, with our hands, the sauce dripping from our chins and to see the utter delight in her face. She, of course, will accompany her meal with a glass of water while I will enjoy a pot of warm saki.

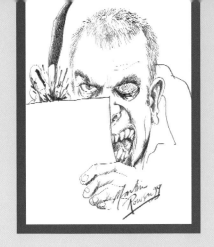

Martin Rowsen

'I'm a cartoonist and writer whose work appears regularly in *The Guardian*, *The Scotsman*, *The Mirror*, *The Express*, *Time Out*, *The Tribune* etc. I've also drawn comic book versions of T.S.Eliot's *The Waste Land* (turned it into an opera) and Sterne's *Tristram Shandy*.'

guests Anna Clark As my wife and best friend, Anna would be my perfect hostess, as well as being around for the post-mortem.

Karl Marx We could make sure his analysis of capitalism inspires a more lasting corrective next Millennium.

Eleanor of Aquitaine Henry II consort... was a formidable and ruthless woman. An excellent role model all in all.

Bugs Bunny He'd be a laugh.

Dorothy Parker Ditto.

Fred Astaire To provide style and grace and some damned good songs between courses.

Katherine Hepburn She played Eleanor of Aquitaine in *The Lion in Winter*, was grossly insulted by Dorothy Parker, and is beautiful and intelligent in great age. She should spark up some interesting conversations.

Darth Vader It would be interesting to see how he'd eat his dinner.

Germaine Greer One of the great cultural liberators, as well as controversialists, of the century.

Gore Vidal As above, only with added bitchiness; (truly, I'd just like to meet Greer and Vidal in real life).

Lucy The prototype australopithecine discovered by the Healeys; she'd affirm the originating matriarchy, despite her probably limited conversation.

location On board the Orient Express travelling between Venice (so we can have a cocktail in Harry's Bar before we leave) and Budapest (for a post-prandial soak in the thermal baths at the Gellent Hotel afterwards).
Why? Have you no sense of romance?

menu Saffron soup. Braised unicorn. Stewed fruit from the tree of Knowledge of Good and Evil (with custard). Cheeses Christ (as it's meant to be his birthday). Drink...lashings of it

music Schubert string quartet, alternating with Fred Astaire singing Cole Porter, Irving Berlin and Gershwin standards.

toast OLD: 'Here's good riddance to a thousand years of Christianity, capitalism, and colonialism (a consequence of both); to the crossest and the cruellest of conflicts, and to a general collective contempt for both our fellow human beings and the other inhabitants with whom we share the Earth.'
NEW: 'Here's to the English Socialist Republic Space Cats!'

seating plan This seating plan seems best to allow the maximum amount of flirting, conversation and rowing–the perfect conditions for a perfect dinner party,

Fred Astaire	Eleanor of Aquitaine	Darth Vader	Dorothy Parker	Me

Anna Clarke | | | | Katherine Hepburn

Karl Marx	Germaine Greer	Bugs Bunny	Lucy	Gore Vidal

Germaine Greer

Karl Marx

Eleanor of Aquitaine

Phil Kearns

Australia's most capped hooker, Phil Kearns staged a remarkable comeback to Test match rugby in 1998, where his leadership and experience helped restore the Wallabies fortunes.

Australian Rugby

guests My father, my mother, my grandfather, my grandmother (Myrtle), my son (Wilson), my next child (not yet born - 3 weeks at 31st December), my wife (Julie), Ron and Jan Marden (father and mother-in-law) – all at my age (32). Me and Julie, at my parents' age, 70.

location My childhood home.

music Nelson Eddy and Janet McDonald - my parents' favourites. Pearl Jam, Seal, REM - my favourites.

toast To generations, to change, to history, to family.

Welsh Rugby

Garin Jenkins

guests My wife, two children, mother and brother.
Kenny Rogers, Eric Clapton and Whitney Houston Brilliant musicians.
Charles Bronson (in *The Great Escape*)
Kirk Douglas as 'Spartacus'.
Billy Connolly For the comedy.
John Wayne (in *True Grit*)
Dr.Who (John Pertwee)

Sophia Loren She will keep John Wayne happy, won't she?
Trevor McDonald

location My caravan.

toast To Jesus Christ - that's why we're celebrating the Millennium after all.

Emile Ntamack

'I'm a rugby player and I play for France. I like life, and I never forget we live only once (not like James Bond!)'

French Rugby

Michael Jordan

Gabriela Sabatini

Bill Gates

Depeche Mode

guests

Philippe Carbonneau, my best friend.
Michael Jordan To understand how we can fly.
Bill Gates To pay for the party.
Al Pacino I like it when he gets upset (after two or three gin and tonics).
Lionel Rossigneux I need a translator; (He speaks Spanish for Gabriela!).
Gabriela Sabatini She's just wonderful and now I've got Lionel Rossigneux.
Depeche Mode They are my favourite band, and I think I can sing with them.
Jim Carey To be sure of a great and funny party.
Marie, of course. She's my wife, my life.

location
In Space, because I want to see the future and the earth and our country.

menu
Champagne, red wine, white wine – Petrus, Sauterne (Yquem)... To eat, just some foie gras on toast.

music
Rap, of course, (Zpac, and Iam) and some Mozart.

toast
No war in the future, then every man might live in peace and love. Good health for everybody. Stop the violence in the streets and help your neighbour. January 1st, 2000, save the children and save ourselves.

S Club 7

Alex Salmond

Kelly Brook

Sandra Bullock

Alex Salmond MP was elected leader of the SNP in 1990, and more than trebled his majority in the 1997 election. In 1999, he was elected to the Scottish parliament and is the leader of the opposition.

guests
Johnny Vaughan
Josh Hartnett
Robbie Williams
Baily from *Party of Five*
Sandra Bullock
Gail Porter [*host*]
Kelly Brook [*host*]
...and everyone all over the world!

location
Wembley Arena, Hyde Park, or New York.

menu
Loads of 7-up (it's our favourite drink), aromatic duck with pancakes, Jamaican patties, mango juice, fruit punch, and chocolate eclairs!

music
Something upbeat: Robbie, party music... anything really.

toast
Cheers! Good health to one and all, and blessed are the cheese makers!

guests
Robert Burns Life and soul of any party – my 'Man of the Millennium'.
William Wallace and **Mel Gibson** So I could introduce them to each other.
Lieutenant Uhuru Boyhood crush.
Joan of Arc My 'Woman of the Millennium'.
Humphrey Bogart and **Lauren Bacall** To see if they made the same electricity off-screen as on-screen.
Catherine Deneuve The 'Face of the Millennium'.

location
Pennan, Aberdeenshire (location of the film, *Local Hero*).

menu
Haggis, neeps and tatties. Whisky and claret.

seating plan
Bogart next to Bacall. Wallace next to Gibson. Salmond next to Uhuru!

music
Something quiet and soft so as not to lose the table talk – maybe Enya.

toast
To humanity.

Gil Scott Heron

For the last thirty years, in his sixteen albums, two novels, two books of poetry and many concerts, lectures and readings, Gil Scott Heron has celebrated strength and survival, protest and empowerment, freedom and revolution, and most of all, the lives of black people.

Billie Holiday

Bob Marley

guests
Don McGriggs
Brian Jackson
Ed Bradey
Larry McDonald
Tony Duncanson
Vernon James
Jimi Hendrix
Billie Holiday
Bob Marley
Johnny Coltrane
1-6 are all members of the band, and I'd invite 7-10 because I've never actually seen any of them play live.

location Stonehenge

menu Anything anyone wanted. I would take orders.

music The music of Bob Marley, Billie Holiday, Johnny Coltrane and Jimi Hendrix.

toast To Peace, 'cos that's something we haven't done yet. To declare a Millennium without conflict. I'd like to see everyone have enough food, to have a roof over their heads and to be able to do what they want to do in life; to open the door to people's dreams; to take away the barriers so that there is the freedom to choose and the chance to achieve what you want to be or what you want to do. To redistribute both wealth and opportunity.

To Peace, cos that's something we haven't done yet

Big Bird

location First I thought about a far away place, like China or France or New Jersey, but then I thought I'd like to have it right on Sesame Street 'cause that's my favourite place in the whole world.

menu Bird seed shakes, peanut butter and bird seed sandwiches with the crusts cut off, boiled bird seed, fried bird seed, bird seed gumbo, bird seed tetrazini, and some bird seed brownies for dessert.

toast If I had a wish for the new Millennium, I wouldn't wish for gold, or money or jewels or even lots of toys; I would just wish for friends, because they are the best gift of all.

music I would like to hear *Fly Robin Fly*, *Wind Beneath My Wings*, *Fly Like an Eagle*, and anything by the Byrds.

Cookie Monster

guests

Mrs. Fields, 'cause me love her cookies.
Famous Amos, cause me love his cookies.
Sarah Lee, cause me love her cookies.
A girl scout, cause me love their cookies.
Seven of Keebler elves, but not just cause me like their cookies, but because they so cute and small, just like their cookies.

menu Me would love to have following

foods: For appetiser me like a nice light cookie, like lemon crème. For salad me like a healthy cookie, like oatmeal raisin. For first course me like hearty cookie, like peanut butter cookie. For main course me like old standard and personal favourite, chocolate chip cookie. For desert me like pie, no on second thought, make that sugar cookie.

toast May your glass of milk on table never run dry and may your cookie in cupboard never crumble!

music Me like the classic cookie rock songs. Like, *He Ain't Heavy, He Me Cookie*, *Take Another Little Piece of Me Cookie*, *In-a-gadda-de-cookie*, and everybody's favourite, *Stairway to Cookie*.

Sesame Street

Sesame Street

Count von Count

toast
May your days be long, so you can count the hours. May your years be many, so you can count the days. And may I always be your friend, so you can count on me.

music
I would like Beethoven's first symphony, Beethoven's second symphony, Beethoven's third symphony, Beethoven's fourth symphony, Beethoven's fifth symphony, Beethoven's sixth symphony, Beethoven's seventh symphony, Beethoven's eighth symphony, Beethoven's ninth symphony, and a Village People album [*host*], so we can dance a little bit.

Bert & Ernie

guests
BERT: We split our guest list up, so I chose six and…

ERNIE: …I chose five.

BERT: Next Millennium you can choose six, Ernie.

ERNIE: Thanks, Bert.

BERT: Here are my guests:

Inventor of the saddle shoe I want to find out how he or she came up with such a brilliant but sensible shoe.

Inventor of oatmeal It's the person that made mornings worth getting up for.

Inventor of the bottle cap To me, they not only invented something to seal in liquid, they also created a beautiful work of art.

Inventor of the paper clip It seems like just a plain, old, ordinary metal wire, yet it's so much more.

Inventor of the tuba To me, the sweetest sound in the world is a tuba blowing in a minor key.

Bernice the pigeon For the conversation.

ERNIE: And here are my guests:

Rubber Duckie 'Cause he's my bath buddy.

Mother Goose 'Cause of all her great rhymes.

Hans Christian Andersen For all his great stories.

Buster Keaton 'Cause he makes me laugh a lot.

Jim Henson 'Cause he was always like a dad to me.

menu
BERT: Well, there'd have to be lots of oatmeal, but none of that fancy oatmeal with sugar and raisins. Just plain oatmeal.

ERNIE: And I'd like food from all over the world like pizza, and tacos and hamburgers and egg rolls and samosas and pad thai and stuff from everywhere.

BERT: Did I mention oatmeal?

Brian Sewell is an art critic for the London *Evening Standard*: 'At the sad end of a once promising career'.

Brian Sewell

guests Michelangelo The greatest of all Renaissance artists.
Giovanni Bernini The greatest of all baroque sculptors.
Schubert Favourite composer.
Richard Strauss Favourite composer.
Wagner Favourite composer.
Titian Favourite painter.
A. J. Ayer He amuses me and would keep the conversation going.
Johannes Wilde My old tutor at the Courtauld Institute.
A. Blunt Old tutor at the Courtauld Institute.
Peter Warlock Curiosity.
Peter Langan Friend.
Plus two live dogs, 22 dead ones, and three cats

location At home.

menu Oysters, prawns, fruits de mer, crab and Chablis.

seating plan In a circle: six move to the left, six to the right at irregular intervals, so that everyone sits next to everyone at some point.

music Schubert songs, sotto voce.

toast To the past.

Schubert

Richard Strauss

two live dogs, 22 dead ones, and three cats

Co-author with Ray Galton...
Steptoe and Son, Hancock's Half Hour, and others too numerous to mention... over 600 in all, plus 7 films and a stage play.

Alan Simpson

Albert Camus

Peter Ustinov

guests

Woody Allen The best comedy talent of my era. The man who, if I wasn't me, I'd rather be.

Albert Einstein I've always wanted to understand his theory of relativity; I couldn't grasp it through Stephen Hawking, but perhaps Albert could explain it over a glass of port.

Will Hay My favourite English film comedian. Also a noted amateur astronomer - something for him to chat to Albert about.

Mozart I'd need someone to give us a tune on the piano afterwards. It was a toss up between him and Charlie Kunz.

Adolf Hitler I've always wanted to ask him just what on earth he was thinking about. Also I'm sure Woody Allen and Albert Einstein would like a few words with him.

Albert Camus A wonderful writer with whom I share a great talent - we were both goalkeepers.

Jacques Tati The only man who ever made me laugh out loud in a cinema, in his superb *Monsieur Hulot's Holiday*.

Johnny Haynes As president of Hampton and Richmond Borough Football Club, I am a football fanatic and Johnny Haynes is the player whose talent gave me more pleasure than any other player I have ever seen.

Peter Ustinov He can talk to all the foreigners in their own language and do the after-dinner speech as well.

Georges Simenon Apart from being my all-time favourite author, I want to find out more about those 10,000 women he reckoned he slept with.

Jennifer Aniston For me, when the others have all gone home. I'm keeping Simenon well away from her – I'll probably have to keep an eye on Mozart as well.

location

Jean-Michel Lorain's La Côte St Jacques, at Joigny – the best restaurant in France and, now that Fredy Girardet has retired, in the world.

menu

Jean-Michel Lorain's Menu Gastronomique - dependent on the morning market.
Bollinger 1928 - the champagne 'the Saint' always drank. Le Montrachet 1982 - the Queen of Burgundies, even though the masculine. Richebourg, Domaine de la Romanée-conti 1952 - the finest red wine I have ever tasted. Chambertin Clos de Beze, Louis Jadot 1976 - beautiful - and I have six cases I'm trying to get rid of. Château d'Yquem 1949 - say no more. Taylor's 1927 - the port of the century. Otard 1820 cognac - my one and only bottle was drunk by my wife and her friends whilst I was away working.
Camp coffee and After Eight mints - I don't want people thinking I'm a snob.

seating plan

Round table, with Alan Simpson at 12 o'clock, and clockwise thereafter: Jennifer Aniston to my left and Will Hay next to her (I can trust him); Einstein next to Will Hay (much physics to discuss); Woody Allen on his left, next George Simenon who is still fuming because he can't get to Jennifer Aniston and has to make do with Mozart to his left. Then comes Peter Ustinov chatting in German to Mozart, and in French and Russian to Jacques Tati on his left. Albert Camus next, discussing the finer points of football with Johnny Haynes on his left and me next to John, joining in while trying to sniff Jennifer Aniston's hair.

toast

To those of us who are still alive, good health. To those of us who are dead, bad luck. And may we all meet here again in 2999, in somebody else's Fantasy Feast.

To those of us who are still alive, good health. To those of us who are dead, bad luck

153

Snooker
Ken Doherty

World Champion snooker player, 1997. 'Easy going and fun loving.'

guests John Lennon • Muhammad Ali • Elvis Presley • Michael Collins • Marilyn Monroe • Frank Sinatra • George Best • William Shakespeare • Albert Einstein • Vincent Van Gogh • Mozart

location Hawaii – one of the most beautiful islands in the world (Ireland excluded).

menu Beluga caviar and Cristal champagne. Fresh, exotic fruits and vegetables with grilled or barbecued seafood. Plenty of exotic cocktails and punch.

seating plan No seats! Everybody would be dancing!

music Rock 'n' roll.

toast A toast to peace, happiness and love ever after. Wipe the slate clean and start afresh in a new, exciting world. No guns, no bombs, only harmony.

George Best

Stephen Hendry

'I am a snooker professional and the current Embassy World Champion. I have won 70 major championships including seven World, six Masters, and five United Kingdom Championships, and I am holder of the most world ranking event titles.

guests Kenny Dalglish • Prince Naseem • Ally McCoist • U2 • Sheryl Crow • Damon Hill • Robert de Niro • The Rolling Stones • Caroline Aherne • Alanis Morrisette • Robbie Williams These are all people I admire a lot and I would love to have a night out with them. I am sure it would be good fun!

location Gleneagles Hotel. It's very posh and very big.

menu Square sausage, chips and beans. Champagne, beer and sparkling mineral water.

music Robbie Williams: *Millennium*

toast Heal the world and make it a better place.

U2

Snooker
Dennis Taylor

'I am a snooker professional who plays in BIG glasses. I was very lucky to have won what people say was the greatest final in the history of the game: 18.5 million viewers watched me pot the final black to win the 1985 Embassy World Championship.'

guests God • The Pope • The Queen • President Clinton • Ian Paisley • Gerry Adams • David Trimble • Martin McGuiness • Tony Blair v John Hulme • Bertie Ahern
All these people sitting down together might be able to solve the Northern Ireland problem! With the help of God!

location A small revolving restaurant with the borders of Northern Ireland and Southern Ireland running through the centre.

menu Irish stew and Guinness.

seating plan A revolving dining table with a smaller table in the middle, revolving in the opposite direction. God would sit at the smaller table in the centre.

music When Irish Eyes Are Smiling.

toast May the next thousand years be a thousand times better than the last.

Mark Williams

'I am a professional snooker player who has been quite successful over the last few years. I reached the Embassy World Championship final this year.'

guests Eddie Izzard Makes me laugh.
Denise Van Outen She's a babe and good fun.
David Duchovny Good actor.
Lisa Kudrow Great in Friends. Girls in Cue Masters offices Always helpful and very friendly.
Robin Williams To dress up as Mrs. Doubtfire.
John Cleese Great actor in Fawlty Towers.
Steps The best group of all time.
Lily Savage Great all-round entertainer.
Richard O'Brien Made the best film ever: The Rocky Horror Show

menu Braised steak and lots of alcohol to wash it down with.

music Queen's Bohemian Rhapsody.

toast I hope in the next Millennium Save the Children continue to be successful in raising funds for such a worthwhile cause.

Robin Williams

Paul Smith

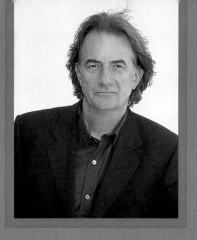

Paul Smith started his career as a gofer in his local clothing warehouse in Nottingham. In 1970 he opened his own shop, and six years later he showed his first collection. Today he has shops all over the world.

guests

Sissy Spacek
David Hockney
Patti Smith
John Lennon
Pauline Denyer-Smith
Bob Dylan
Tracey Scholfield
Bob Marley
Tracey McCleod

location The grounds of Eltham Hall in Derbyshire. As a child, I visited the grounds of this hall often, and as a teenager I used to cycle there from my home town of Nottingham – consequently, I have fond memories of it!

menu Wine: Red (something from Piemonte); white (Chablis premier cru) Food based on the colour green, to match the location!

music Music from Woodstock.

toast Excellent old one; brilliant new one.

Bob Dylan

Soul 2 Soul Jazzie B

Soul 2 Soul became globally famous in the late eighties with the single *Back to Life*.

guests

Mrs S.
Aitch
Daddae
Q
Nelson

Wally Baker
Bob Marley
Malcolm X
Martin Luther King
Murkely
Kim

location Antigua, Half Moon Bay.

menu Fish and chicken barbecue, salad, Coco bread champagne, punch, beer, water

seating plan Everyone jump up - no seating.

music Nuff music - me as DJ

toast No toast

Once Mayor of Cincinnati, Jerry Springer now hosts his own controversial talk show, The Jerry Springer Show.

For the next thousand years, take care of yourself...and each other.

Oprah Winfrey

Thomas Jefferson

guests

Abraham Lincoln

Robert F. Kennedy

Thomas Jefferson

Winston Churchill

Frank Sinatra

Roger Maris

Babe Ruth

William Shakespeare

Robert de Niro

Oprah Winfrey

Adolf Hitler (so I can poison him)

location   Yankee Stadium.

menu   Burgers, fries, chocolate chip cookies, and diet cola.

music   Elvis Presley and Frank Sinatra.

toast   We stand here on the crest of time, and as twilight fades on the 20th Century. I am in awe of all that mankind has accomplished in the last thousand years – how far we have come from the barbaric days of senseless wars, religious persecution and ethnic hatred. Indeed, how far *have* we come?

My hope for the new Millennium is that the lessons of the past are not soon forgotten.

That with all our scientific advances we evolve to become better people, as well. May we finally know a world of compassion, love, and respect for our fellow man...as well as for the delicate balance of life that surrounds us.

Now, as the impending dawn of a new Millennium approaches, the thought occurs to me that we have come a long way. One thousand years ago, as our predecessors

faced the turn of the Millennium, they feared, with indescribable panic, that the year 1000 would bring with it the coming of the final judgement day – the end of the world. Today, I am merely worried about whether or not my internet server will be functioning tomorrow. Now that's progress. Here's to tomorrow, and the unlimited possibilities it brings. For the next thousand years, take care of yourself...and each other.

Bill Stott

DAMIEN HIRST'S FANTASY FEAST

WINNER'S DINNERS after . . . . . .

FANTASY FEAST 2000? BAD FOOD IS BAD FOOD!

A poor Yorkshire pudding.

INSET: BAD FILMS ARE BAD FILMS

Ian Stark

Aged Olympian equestrian - seen better days but still kicking!!

guests

My wife I wouldn't like to go into 2000 without her.

The Queen Because she is everything British and I rather like her.

Paul McCartney To represent all 'veggies' and make him eat and enjoy rare British beef on the bone.

Michelle Pfeiffer Just to say 'miaoww' in her cat suit.

Clive James Fun and interesting to chat to.

Victor Meldrew Because I'm going to be like him later in life!!

Dame Kiri Te Kanawa So she could sing to me!

Mr Bean To make me cringe and laugh at his antics.

Henry VIII To discuss his wives and his ideals.

Stephanie Stark and **Timothy Stark** My children – they are the best entertainment.

location
Hawaii, with waitresses in straw skirts on the beach.

menu
Seafood salad starter. British beef on the bone (very rare, running blood). Sticky toffee pudding (my favourite). Lots of vintage champagne and 'serious' red wine.

music
Every type of music would be played throughout the evening, from classical to rap. At midnight I would play Beethoven's 1812.

toast
How life has changed in the past thousand years. Improved? I wonder. I toast that the world as we know it, still exists in 3000.

Candi Staton

"Happy"!

guests

Jesus Christ He'd be there first.

J.F. Kennedy I always admired him; he was a great man. I think he was one of the greatest Presidents we've ever had and I would love to be in his presence.

Marilyn Monroe

My mother She passed away in 1979. She would definitely be there.

My father He is also deceased. I'd have them both at my Millennium party.

Aretha Franklin

Afriden Simpson

Eddie Murphy He's funny.

Robin Williams He's funny too.

Chris Rock He's good.

Bugs Bunny Why not?

James Bond Roger Moore - he's cool.

location
In Paris – we can dance all night in the street.

menu
Lots of Pina Colada and sparkling apple cider; I don't drink alcohol anymore but if they wanted to drink, that's fine with me – let them do it!

seating plan
J.F. Kennedy and Marilyn would sit next to each other – after all, it's a party!

music
My dance music, of course – we'd all be dancing in the street listening to *La La Love* and *Girl's Run Free*.

toast
I'd give a toast to the old, and I would toast the brand new coming in with lots of new ideas.

Aretha Franklin

Through many books, including *I Leonardo*, *Sigmund Freud* and *the Big I Am*, *The Story of God*, I have realised that I am a visual pragmatist, an anarchist, a royalist and a contradictor of my own beliefs and ideas. It is so much more fun than to believe the same damn thing throughout a life.

Ralph Steadman

guests **Friedrich Nietzsche** He said 'We possess art, lest we perish from the truth'.

Picasso He had all the fun.

Marcel Duchamp Biggest influence on our concept of art, and maintains it still.

Marianne Faithful Her voice has a lived-in quality, she is fun to talk to and has been around at least twice.

Hunter S.Thompson 'Cos he's my buddy! He generates energy and energy is LIFE.

Penelope Wilton Great actress and effervescent personality.

Leonardo da Vinci The man who woke up in the dark and had a telephone number before the phone was invented.

Jonathan Swift For the spice of bone-scraping satire to remind us all that we are always at our worst.

Jodie Foster Her self control, animal stealth, charisma, mystery and the vulnerable impediment in the sound of her voice.

Dennis Healey The man who would have seen Maggie off and helped us all to believe in a UK with a human face.

My wife, Anna For her composure, her beauty, her organising skills, her reassurance and above all, my love for her.

location Machu Picchu, southern Andes in Peru; centre of Inca's universe and last citadel of Inca resistance against the Spanish. They studied rainbows, bird flight, earthquakes and the dung of llamas for omens. This is the Millennium spot to be and it the end is indeed nigh it would give us a granstand view of the last dawn.

Jodie Foster

Pablo Picasso

Penelope Wilton

Friedrich Nietzsche

I am a visual pragmatist, an anarchist, a royalist and a contradictor of my own beliefs and ideas

menu Coca leaves wrapped around peacock pate and Mescal aperitif for altitude sickness. Angel fish delicately grilled on the finest shivers. Politicians' buttocks as a starter, garnished in Spin Doctor kidney and wine sauce. T–bone tiger steak as main dish with 238 varieties of potato common to Peru in every conceivable variation. Breast of Snowshoe Rabbit steam-cooked in white Meursault Burgundy inside fresh bamboo shoots. Gallons of Château Petrus, 1945.

seating plan Auditorium semicircle of guests. Order immaterial save for chemical attraction and personal preference. If someone cannot agree they will be thrown 2000 feet down into Urubamba river – and miss the fun.

music Aaron Copland's *Fanfare for the Common Man* and Beethoven's *Missa Solemnis* with Spike Milligan's *I'm Walking Backwards for Christmas*, and Spike Jones' *Cocktails for Two*.
Vaughan Williams' *Satan's Dance of Triumph* from Job, William Breuker–Haydn *Concerto for Trumpet*. Finish on theme music from Stanley Kubrick's *2001* as the sun rises, orchestrated with Bob Dylan's *It's alright ma, I'm only bleeding*.

toast It is only at such a place as this that we can contemplate Nietzsche's statement between madman and Zarathrustra, his pagan prophet, who declared 'It is only as an aesthetic phenomenon that existence and the world are permanently justified'. I have brought you all here to witness that phenomenon in the dawn of a new Millennium. The sun is about to rise and reveal new possibilities, to light the corners and crevices, to illuminate and dispel the ghosts of all our fears, inside what I choose to call the 'Land of God's Own Laboratory'. We are sitting on 'The Ancient Summit', the 'last hitching place of the SUN', and for this short but precious time we can feel like gods contemplating our pasts and our futures as time catches breath on its own threshold. Drink up and embrace a New World which you can see spread out beyond. To the next 1000 years.

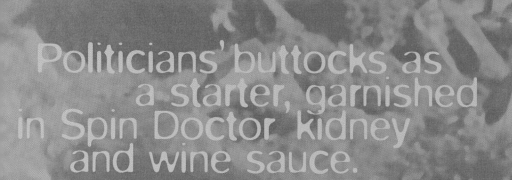

Politicians' buttocks as a starter, garnished in Spin Doctor kidney and wine sauce.

Jackie Stewart

Motor-racing driver, Jackie Stewart started in 99 races and won 27 world championship races between 1965 and 1973. He was world champion three times and retired at the end of 1973 to take up a career in broadcasting. He is also and expert at clay pigeon shooting and has come close to Olympic selection.

guests King Hussein
Probably the most remarkable man I've ever met. He was a good friend.
Sir Peter Ustinov [host]
My wife
David Niven
Sean Connery
Billy Connolly

All the above because they are or were friends and all great conversationalists.
My two sons
George Harrison
The Princess Royal
Fangio
The above three all friends.

location In my home…because that's my environment.

menu A good champagne, a good red wine, and a good Scottish water.

music The Beatles playing live – all their wonderful songs, including *Sgt.Pepper* in the run-up to the Millennium, and some of their softer numbers at dinner.

David Niven

Fangio

Peter Ustinov

Sean Connery

Shelley von Strunckel

Love, learning and leaving something good behind (and sharing these with others) matter most. As an astrologer, whether it's writing in London's *Sunday Times*, or publications worldwide,fund raising for the Red Cross, or entertaining friends, my aim is to bring hope and lift others' spirits.

I've invited a combination of mystics and cynics. As hostess, I love to hear people who wouldn't otherwise meet, explore each other's viewpoint – always intrigued, occasionally clashing, and sometimes becoming best of friends.

guests Nostradamus He'd be fascinating company. And, I'd be dying to learn how the man, whose predictions dazzle the world with their accuracy, did it. I want to hear his view of the state of affairs here on earth now and the prognosis for our future.

Sam Taylor Wood

Artist.

guests Jay Jopling My gorgeous husband. No dinner is complete without him.
Buddha For spiritual guidance.
Marlon Brando For spot-on impersonations of Marlon Brando.
Caravaggio For artistic guidance, and he was a bit of a party animal.
Jesus To tell us what God is really like, and for great stories.
Pier Paolo Pasolini To film the event.

Marilyn Monroe To put to bed the mystery.
John Kennedy Jr. To see him again.
David Beckham To look at.
Medici
Henry VIII To make sure the party is a party.

location The Ivy in London - everyone goes to celebrity-watch, and this will blow their socks off!

menu Sushi, lots of sake and chips, then sticky toffee pudding.

music Music from *the Last Castrato* - Alessandro Morecchi,

toast To all those who aimed low in life...and missed.

Marlon Brando

David Beckham

The Ivy... everyone goes to celebrity-watch, and this will blow their socks off!

Voltaire He would lend the witty tongue of a great writer, and stimulate the conversation by lending perspective to others' pronouncements.
Merlin What wonders he could tell us about unseen worlds, both within us and around us.
Noel Coward Every party needs someone with a dry sense of humour and quick wit to lighten the mood when things turn serious, and to be serious when the mood's become overly frivolous.
Benjamin Franklin American wit and wisdom, and, according to legend, a student of astrology as well.
Nigel Gerald My husband, whose capacity

to be charming is balanced by his quick barrister's wit.
P. D. James Her skill with words and pungent view of humanity's foibles would help remind us of what we are at our worst and what we need to overcome to be our best.
Hildegard von Bingen Best known today for her choral music (which will be sung), she was one of the 12th century's great minds, a revolutionary within the Church, and she touched every element of society.
Dorothy Parker Her irreverent quips would keep the group from taking anything - including themselves - too seriously.
Evangeline Adams The American

astrologer who advised millionaires such as Carnegie, and challenged laws that viewed astrologers as fortune tellers .
Jane Austen She still cannot be topped for perspective on life, love, and a loving but uncompromising view of human quirks.

toast To a future in which we will: Carry with us all the wisdom, perspective and joy of the years past (knowledge mellowed with compassion); and leave behind our inhumanity, pains, wars and persecutions; and each day develop a closer relationship with the Divinity that created us, illustrating it by our humanity to others and kindness to ourselves.

Texas

Sharleen Spiteri

Singer / songwriter for Texas

Richard Burton and Elizabeth Taylor

John Lennon and Paul McCartney

Five fantastic couples...
John and Jackie Kennedy,
Paul McCartney and John Lennon,
Richard Burton and Elizabeth Taylor,
Charlotte and Emily Bronte,
Robin Hood and Maid Marion

guests Five fantastic couples:
John and Jackie Kennedy
Paul McCartney and John Lennon
Richard Burton and Elizabeth Taylor
Charlotte and Emily Bronte
Robin Hood and Maid Marion
Eddie Spiteri, my dad – to help ease
conversation with tales of the high seas,
and to step in if things kick off.

location Glasgow Art Gallery, before a
big night out on the town.

menu Turkey roast, and veggie nut
roast for Macca and Robin Hood.

music No background sound, although
Lennon, McCartney and Maid Marion could
head a Hogmanay sing-a-long later.

seating plan Free seating

toast No man is an island.

Margaret Thatcher

toast

My toast for the next Millennium is a wish: that cruelty to children should be no more and that their suffering could be banished. What joy that would bring us all and what greater hope we could have for the generations that follow.

Iwan Thomas

Welsh 400 metres runner:
'Energetic, kind, friendly, honest.'

guests   Homer Simpson He's funny – would liven up any party.
Princess Diana Would have loved to meet her.
Robbie Williams So he could entertain us!
Samuel L Jackson He's just a superb actor.
Jack Dee He seems a bit grumpy but he's very funny. He'd be the man.
Jesus Ask for some of his powers so I could take them on to the running track with me. I think that's what I'd go for.

Muhammad Ali He's just a legend.
Bruce Lee Without a doubt...because he died in quite dodgy circumstances, he's just a legend, and I love his Kung Fu films.
Will Smith He's just brilliant.
Marilyn Monroe Because I need a babe at the party, and I could also ask her why she was murdered – or at least what she was up to.
Nostradamus To ask him what my future holds for me!

location   In my apartment – I've just decorated it.

menu   Massive variety of everything...so there was food that everyone would like.

seating plan   I would like it to be a revolving table.. with everyone changing seats every twenty minutes..

toast   To the future!

165

Joanna Trollope

'Novelist, 5'9" tall, fair, size 6 feet, extremely short sighted, all her own teeth (so far…)'

guests

Geoffrey Chaucer For cleverness, benevolence, and humour.

Jane Lapotaire For originality, charm, and guts.

Captain Corelli For sex appeal.
The young Marlon Brando For ditto.

George Eliot For brains.

Charles II For vigour, appetites, and party spirit.

Mary Kingsley For courage and wit.

Elizabeth Bennet For spirit and sparkle.

Kiri Te Kanawa For beauty and voice.

An Archangel For spiritual presence and dignity.

Marco Polo For the stories.

location

On a terrace on a perfect night, above a perfect valley in Tuscany or Umbria, with no mosquitoes.

menu

Everybody would bring something from their period or their place. So the menu would vary from Restoration fantasies from Charles II to a little manna de luxe from the archangel.

seating plan

We'd move round with each course, to share each other out. I like the idea of George Eliot being, at one point, between Marlon Brando and Charles II; they'd both probably take a shine to her.

music

I'd get Kiri to sing all her favourites from *Manhattan* to Mozart.

toast

May we take the best, with humility and gratitude, from the past, and endeavour to profit from it, for the future.

Marlon Brando

Kiri Te Kanawa

Charles II

166

Pete Tong

guests Marilyn Monroe She'd have to sing me a song!

Steve McQueen Our driver!

Debs Tong My wife…or I'll be in trouble.

Alfred Hitchcock He could do the horror-scopes.

Bob Marley The band!

Kate Moss To keep her out of trouble; she could bring some friends too.

Carl Cook Our DJ.

Audrey Hepburn So we could wonder at her beauty and set Breakfast at Tiffany's the next day.

David Bailey [host] Some one has to take the snaps!

Jennifer Lopez Our dancer!

Liz Hurley She'd keep out Hello!

location The Lost City or Atlantis…well nobody around here has ever been there!

menu Milk, honey, nectar, and large fries please.

music Wait and see – come and see me at Cream, or turn on your radio!

As well as DJ'ing in clubs all across the world, Pete Tong hosts a show on Radio 1 every friday night. He is also the director of A & R for the record label FFRR.

Phil Tufnell

Cricketer - the England selectors

guests

Paul Whitehouse
To tell us funny stories all night.

Cindy Crawford Fit bird.

Robbie Williams To sing us a song.

Howard Marks Good story teller.

Robin Smith He's my mate! and we could talk a little bit about cricket.

Catherine Zeta Jones Another fit bird.

Iggy Pop Cool tunes and top nutter.

Marilyn Monroe Everybody's favourite lady.

Steve McQueen Cool dude.

Joanna Lumley To add a bit of class.

George Best A legend.

location Doyle's, on the beach - Sydney, Australia. Lovely Aussie people; top spot on cool beach.

menu Seafood – Doyle's has the best! Lots of Chardonnay.

seating plan Rectangular table : Self at head of table right and clockwise as follows: Cindy Crawford, Robbie Williams, Marilyn Munroe, Steve McQueen, George Best, Howard Marks (at opp. head of table), Iggy Pop, Robin Smith, Joanna Lumley, Paul Whitehouse, Catherine Zeta Jones.

music Bob Marley and dance music.

toast Be your own MAN.

Peter Ustinov

Sir Peter Ustinov is an actor and writer. He has starred in more than 35 films and has won two Oscars. He has written plays, books and film scripts and has directed plays, films and operas.

guests Helene Ustinov, my wife – for being as independent as myself.
Tamara, my eldest daughter – for her talent, and her instinct for life.
Pavla, my daughter – for her beauty, and her sense of the absurd.
Igor, my son – a fine sculptor taking our name into the next Millennium.
Andrea, my youngest daughter – for her robust sense of fun and piercing intelligence.

Ernest Bevin, A great and wonderful man.
Nelson Mandela, For his humanity and great wisdom.

location My home in Switzerland.

menu Vichyssoise. Caviar and Blini. A large but simple salmon with the freshest array of seasonal vegetables. A complete selection of French cheeses. To drink – the best my vineyard has produced.

Nelson Mandela

To drink – the best my vineyard has produced.

ITS SHERLOCK HOLMES. HE WANTS TO THANK YOU FOR THE INVITATION THAT YOU ARE JUST ABOUT TO WRITE HIM...

Richard Tomes

Ed Victor

Born in New York, have lived in London for 35 years. Worked for Weidenfield and Nicolson, Jonathan Cape before establishing own literary agency in 1976. Clients include: Kathy Lette, Douglas Adams, Frederick Forsyth and Jack Higgins. On the board of the Almeida Theatre, Arts Foundations and London Literary Festival.

guests

Oscar Wilde
Odysseus
Carol Ryan (my wife)
Marlene Dietrich
Iris Murdoch
Kathy Lette [*host*]
Lenny Bruce
Mel Brooks
Christopher Marlowe
Arthur Ashe
Jane Austen

location
The Gritti Palace, Venice. I would like to be in a place where things were happening 1000 years ago and Venice was thriving. Venice is a city of fantasy.

menu
Mountains of caviar with 1990. Cristal champagne. Choice of mixed grilled fish / meats from the Monaco Gran Canale Hotel, green noodles from Harry's Bar. and Château Latour to drink. Tiramisu. 1900 Armagnac.

seating plan

music
Glen Gould playing the Goldberg variations of Bach quietly in the corner.

toast
Remembering all those we have loved who did not live to celebrate with us this evening, and hoping for peace, health and happiness for all of us who are going forward into the next Millennium.

Christopher Marlowe · Marlene Dietrich · Ed Victor · Mel Brooks · Jane Austen · Arthur Ashe · Lenny Bruce · Carol Ryan · Odysseus · Iris Murdoch · Oscar Wilde · Kathy Lette

Oscar Wilde

Marlene Dietrich

Village People

VILLAGE PEOPLE

Village People has been entertaining audiences since 1977. Their hits, *YMCA*, *Macho Man*, *In the Navy*, *Can't Stop the Music*, *Go West*, *San Fransisco/In Hollywood* and more, have sold over 65 million records and CD's worldwide. Their six characters – Cop, Indian, Cowboy, Construction Worker, G.I.(Military) and Biker – are instantly recognisable as the most fun party band in the world.
Left to right: David Hodo - 'the Construction Worker'; Ray Simpson - 'the Cop'; Felipe Rose - 'the American Indian'; Jeff Olson - 'the Cowboy'; Alexander Briley - 'the Military Rep'; Glenn Hughes - 'the Biker / Leatherman'

L'Chaim. To life. How do I look?

guests J.S. Bach • Albert Einstein • Ghengis Khan • Chaka Khan • Jesus Christ • Marilyn Monroe • Iris Chacon • Jacqueline Kennedy Onassis • George • Washington Carver • Dag Hammersjold • Mary Pickford • Ava Gardner • Julius Ceasar

location
The Taj Mahal

menu Thai/Tex-Mex food. Thai beer, Singha beer, Cristal champagne, Pelegrino water.

music

David:	Square Dance from 'Voyage'
Felipe:	Lauryn Hill
Alex:	Dvorjak
Jeff:	Innagoddadavida by Iron Butterfly
Ray:	Reach Out and Touch by Ashford and Simpson
Glenn:	Swing music

toast L'Chaim. To life. How do I look?

J. S. Bach

Jacqueline Kennedy Onassis

Ava Gardner

Ghengis Khan

Virgin radio

Chris Evans

guests Jo Guest • Homer Simpson • Danny Baker • Johnny Boy

location In my kitchen.

menu Curry. Any alcohol.

music Van Morrison: *Back on Top*.

toast To all the women in the world who put up with us men - God bless you.

John Revell

guests Tommy Cooper • Eric Morecambe • Chris Evans • Bridget Bardot • Holly Samos

location The Guinness factory in Dublin.

menu Chickity China the Chinese chicken. Guinness and Bollinger champagne.

music My CD collection.

toast Here's to the next 100 beers.

Holly Samos

guests Paul McCartney • John Lennon • Steve McQueen • Paul Newman • Robert Redford • My mother • Huey from Fun Lovin' Criminals • Elvis Presley • Frank Sinatra • Dean Martin • The Queen Mother • My Nan • Madonna • My sister, Lisa

location A small island in the South Pacific with sea views and beautiful weather.

menu Champagne, and vodka Red Bulls to keep us up. Meze food – lots of dishes across the table rather than your own plate full – including fish, meat and vegetable dishes plus some Greek dips, Greek salad, cheese pie, moussaka and chips!

seating plan Steve McQueen would be seated next to me!!

toast Peace, health and happiness.

Steve McQueen

Jamie Broadbent

guests The Simpsons • Bob Marley • John Lennon • Frank Sinatra • Cameron Diaz • Kate Moss • And my close mates and family

location In the snug of the local pub in Jamaica.

music The Beatles.

toast A schlu ver daar a hharrr.

Dan McGrath

guests Prince • Robbie Williams • Jarvis Cocker • U2 So they can sing their topical turn-of-century songs. **Nik Goodman** Head of music programming at Virgin Radio.

location Round at mine.

menu Seafood and Bollinger RD 1975

toast I wonder what we'll be doing this time next year?

San and Tray (from Viz)

I'm San. Sandra Burke. I'm 26 an' I've 'ad more bangs than she's 'ad hot dinners.

I'm Tracy Tunstall. I'm 26 an' I've 'ad fifteen hot dinners...today!

guests Baz 'Cos he'll give us a lift 'ome in his motorbike and sidecar, if it's still working because of the Millennium bug. Dave 'Cos he's Baz's best mate. Peter Andre 'Cos he's got an Atlantic Ripple and a six–pack. Adam Rickitt [*host*] 'Cos he's got an Atlantic Ripple and a six–pack. The Chippendales 'Cos they've got Atlantic Ripples and six–packs. The bloke from the Off–licence 'Cos he's got a Cadbury's Ripple and a Party Seven. Linford Christie 'Cos he's got a massive lunchbox that he keeps his genitals in. Leonardo di Caprio 'Cos he was lush in Titanic. George Clooney 'Cos he was lush in E.R.

The bloke in the 11.30 appointment advert 'Cos he was lush in the 11.30 appointment advert. And he's got an Atlantic Ripple and a six–pack. Jesus Christ So as he could turn water into Malibu and coke.

location The 'Dog and Hammer' at the end of our street. We can walk 'ome from there 'cos taxis are going to be a thousand quid...an' there's a Pernod promotion on Millennium night.

menu Chips, curry sauce, pork scratchings. Pernod, Taboo, and a drink on a stick off Baz.

seating plan Rectangular table with San and Tray sitting with the grub at one end and everybody else at the other end with a bowl of salad. The bar situated at the end where San and Tray are sitting.

music Agadoo (Black Lace), *The Birdie Song* (The Tweets), *Superman* (Black Lace), *We're Havin' a Gang Bang* (Black Lace).

toast The last 1000 years have been a time of immense change, a period of upheaval, unprecedented in the annals of history. It seems only appropriate that on this unique occasion, we pause to reflect on...hey, Look! They're taking the clingfilm off the buffet!

The Chippendales... 'cos they've got Atlantic Ripples and six–packs

The Chippendales

Adam Rickitt

George Clooney

Leonardo di Caprio

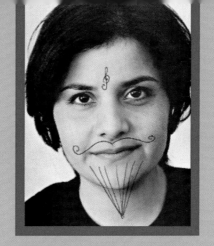

One of the stars of *Goodness Gracious Me.*
DESCRIBE YOURSELF IN 50 WORDS: 'I can't; 0 words would not near cover what I have achieved in my lifetime, or, indeed, in my adolescence. I mean, really... actress, comedienne, writer, performer, dancer, singer, choreographer, interior designer... doesn't even cover my pre-teens. Oh bollocks, is that 50 already?'

Nina Wadia

guests My mum She'd slap me if I didn't invite her.
Joan Rivers The first lady of stand-up comedy. She'd get along great with guest no. 9 (Whoever wrote *The Kama Sutra*).
Jackie Chan If I could get him drunk enough, he might just fight my next guest. Ooh, what a treat!
Bruce Lee I'd feel protected and loved.

Antoine de Caunes I fancy a bit of French.
Pete He lives next door.
Johnny Bravo [*host*] The sexiest cartoon character I've ever seen.
Stanley Kubrick To ask him why he never gave me a walk-on part in *Eyes Wide Shut*.
Whoever wrote *The Kama Sutra* Imagine the conversation...'But how do you get your leg to do that?'

Ricky Martin I feel sorry for him; he's probably not been invited elsewhere.
My husband, Raiomond Mirza. It would be rude not to invite him.

location My flat. I will convert it to look like a huge perfume bottle! What fun!

menu I would invite the Maharaja from *Goodness Gracious Me* to cater – including exotic dishes such as tiger's bum on a cracker and monkey brain soup. For the vegetarians a huge fish from Mani. Drinks would include 7 Up.

seating plan A mirror would enable all the guests in the semi-circle to talk freely with everyone and keep an eye on the waiters, which would include Tony Blair (he asked – he's running a bit low on the cash front). Guest no. 11 (husband) would be a bit squashed but it can't be helped. He's near the spout, er, toilets.

music I will be debuting my new single, *Nina and the Millennium – 2000 and me –* sort of about my ex-boyfriends.

toast Ode to the Millennium-Oh, Millennium! Alas, you are to be no more. Oh well... personally, I hated the 1900's. But, 'tis not to be feared, You will return again, next year, Well, a bit longer really. Thanks for the tears and the joy. Well, actually, only the joy; the tears really hurt, man. Good-bye to the old. Hello to the new.

Hello.
Nina

Terry Waite

Terry Waite CBE, has worked and travelled throughout the world. He was an advisor to the 102nd Archbishop of Canterbury and was locked up in the Middle East for almost five years. He now writes, broadcasts, lectures and is involved with many charities.

guests

William McGonagall He thought of himself as one of the world's greatest poets. Regrettably, few others did. At intervals during the meal William would be invited to recite extracts from his works. He would, of course, have written a special ode for this occasion and would recite it after guests had consumed several bottles of claret.

Henry VIII As he had such a dreadful domestic life, he might welcome an evening away from home.

The Bishop of London An old friend and colleague of mine who would give King Henry a run for his money.

One of my captors from Beirut I would like him to see that everything in life is not so gloomy as he might imagine. He, of course, could remain anonymous but would be invited to disclose his identity at midnight, when all would be forgiven.

Harry Houdini He will be invited to sing for his supper and will no doubt be able to surprise the gentleman from Beirut with one or two tricks.

Sir Maurice Oldfield Former head of M16 who will be expected to show total indiscretion and regale the company with stories of his exploits.

Sir Winston Churchill Providing he does not hog the conversation. He might be a good counter-balance for Henry.

Britannia There ought to be some ladies and, according to our respected leaders, she is the coolest one around. She could leave her toasting fork behind unless she intends to stay for breakfast.

Lucretia Borgia She would add a touch of excitement to the proceedings, especially when we dip our spoons into a rather dull Brown Windsor soup.

Queen Victoria Invited out of mere curiosity, to see if she might be amused by the evening.

John Brown Invited out of mere curiosity also, to see if he might be amused by the evening.

location

The Dining Room of the Travellers' Club, known by members as The Coffee Room – the setting for many fantasy functions since the early 1800's.

menu

Brown Windsor soup. Roast beef on the bone; Crisp roast potatoes; Assorted vegetables. Steamed apple pudding and cream. Stilton and other British cheeses. Coffee. Champagne, claret, liquers

seating plan

Reasons for seating plan: William McGonagall to sit in the middle, so that he can bore everyone equally. One of my captors from Beirut to sit next to Lucretia Borgia, just to see how sharp he really is. The Bishop of London to keep the conversation going at that end of the table.

music

The Band of the Grenadier Guards will play in the garden before and after the meal. Definitely no music will be played during the meal. At the stroke of midnight, following the national anthem, McGonegall will play *Dr. Robert Runcie MC* on the bagpipes – a tune composed especially for the bagpipes for my former employer, and rarely played. We shall remember him with great affection on this occasion, as we welcome in the new Millennium.

Henry VIII

Queen Victoria	Britannia
Bishop of London	Harry Houdini
William McGonegall	Sir Winston Churchill
John Brown	One of Beirut captors
Sir Maurice Oldfield	Lucretia Borgia

Terry Waite

toast

May this feast of the resurrection bring us hope, joy, and peace. May we step towards the morrow with a cheerful heart and may God have mercy on all our many failings.'

Winston Churchill

As a designer, my philosophy has always been to create clothes that give the wearer confidence and make them feel special through flattering cut, and luxurious feel.

Amanda Wakeley

Dalai Lama

Billy Connolly

Tom Cruise

Mozart

guests

Jesus Christ Why not?

The Dalai Lama Why not?

Bruce Webber (photographer) For his extraordinary vision of people through the lens of a camera; and so to record the feast.

Sylvie Guillem (dancer) For some pre-dinner entertainment.

Billy Connolly To keep the conversation down-to-earth and exceptionally funny.

Kathy Lette [*host*] The female version of Billy Connolly.

Mozart To meet a true genius who apparently had a sense of humour too.

Goldie Hawn (a) For amusement factor. (b) To hear some of her beauty secrets.

Tom Cruise and **Nicole Kidman** They fascinate me as a couple.

My lover (and no, you can't know his identity) Isn't that obvious?

location
A beach on a south sea island, as close as possible to the rising sun – to be one of the first to see in the new Millennium.

menu
A feast of local exotic seafood and fruits and the bitterest Belgian chocolate! Louis Roederer Cristal to drink.

seating plan
Guests seated on cushions on the beach around a large, low, round table; but no seating plan necessary as guests would circulate throughout the evening.

music
Mike Oldfield's *Tubular Bells* – a modern classic.

toast
Let mankind unite to make this world a better place for the next Millennium.

Fay Weldon

Fay Weldon's first novel *The Fat Woman's Joke* was published in 1967. Since then she has written over twenty novels and many radio and television plays.

guests Thackeray A good conversationalist and a skilled writer.
Scott Fitzgerald Ditto above.
Martin Luther To keep the above two in order.
The Duchess of Devonshire Beautiful and bright.
Jay McInenney To get on with Scott Fitzgerald.
Princess Di To get on with the Duchess of Devonshire.
The Bishop of Edinburgh So Martin Luther would have someone to get on with.
Cherie Blair To give us some gossip on the here and now.
Peter Mandelson To be the fly in everyone's ointment.
Marilyn Monroe To relax and charm everyone.
Jane Austen To take notes.

location The Ivy – you can forget where you are, and people are used to celebrities.

Cherie Blair

Martin Luther King

Princess Diana

menu Some of these guests will have weak digestion; some, like Luther, won't want excess. We'll have good Californian Merlot to drink. The conversation will be more important than the food. Everyone will want something different – Monroe will eat salad; Luther will eat boiled potatoes; the indulgent can have suckling pig; the Ivy's Caramelised Onion Tart for some; Caesar salad for others; steak for the brave; fish for the pure; ice-cream. For Luther, a surprise; for the Duchess of Devonshire, a treat. But who am I to say what they'll eat? I'll just pay the bill.

music Mozart, I think. For all tastes, old and new, a little Country and Western music.

toast
Here's to the past that we remember
Here's to the future that we don't
Here's to the present, because that's all we have.

Cherie Blair... to give us some gossip on the here and now

Author of The *Acid House* and *Trainspotting*: 'I'm pretty fantastic, but so are most people. I've been able to make a decent living out of underachieving.'

Irvine Welsh

guests Sid Vicious A punk hero.
Mother Theresa Won't eat too much – more for me and Elvis.
Elvis Presley Rock 'n' roll hero.
Iggy Pop Living God.
Pat Stanton All-time great.
Princess Diana
Jim Baxter Lend a hand with the bevy.
Jock Scott All-time great and could also lend a hand with the bevy.
Benny Brazil To see him play was quite a thrill.
George Best [*host*] He'll help us get through the champagne.
Rommell (Field Marshall) Top dress sense – 'the first mod'.

location Dizzy Lizzies Lounge Bar, Buchanan St, Leith, Edinburgh – equidistant of all cultural amenities.

menu Egg and chips, pie, beans, sausage rolls, assortment of curries provided by Tommy Mia's Raj Restaurant. Champagne, lager, purple tin (Tennents Superlager).

music Lenny D. would provide all the music on an ear-splitting sound system.

toast Farewell old Millennium some of it was shite some of it alright. Hello new Millennium I expect much the same yet again

George Best

Iggy Pop

Rommell

Sid Vicious

Ann Widdecombe

guests Charles II To watch interaction with No.2 (Lucy Walters) and decide if they did marry.
Lucy Walters To watch with No.1 (Charles II).
Friar Tuck I love to watch my guests enjoy their food.
Jane Austen To make witty reflections on her fellow guests.
Rudolph Rassendyll What a dish!
Little Gda Deserves a treat. And no table is complete at celebrations without a child.
John Buchan To entertain the guests with stories.
Mrs Doasyouwouldbedoneby To make us all happy.
Saint Peter To remind us what the celebrations are all about.
Agatha Christie To add mystery.
Basil Brush [*host*] To keep him safe from the hunt.

location A large conservatory overlooking a Scottish Loch.

menu Tomato soup. Beef on the bone, Yorkshire puddings, three good English vegetables (no Islington nonsense), horseradish, mustard, and roast potatoes. Pear pavlova; cheese and biscuits; coffee and mints.

seating plan (Rectangular table) Friar Tuck opposite Saint Peter, to learn better ways. Charles II next to Lucy Walters, for reason above. Jane Austen other side of Charles II, and next to Rudolph Rassendyll, so she can compare a fictional hero to a real one. Basil Brush at end. Little Gda next to him so he can entertain her. Mrs Doasyouwouldbedoneby next to little Gda. John Buchan opposite Charles II and next to Agatha Christie, so they can swap yarns. Me at the end.

toast To His Church in His third Millennium.

Saint Peter

Basil Brush

Jane Austen

Editor of *The New Statesman*. Former editor of *The Independent on Sunday*, and a former education correspondent with *The Observer*, and *The Times*.

Westlife

guests Everybody who works for *Smash Hits*, everybody who has helped us be successful, and everybody who supports us!

location A very big place – maybe a castle in Ireland.

menu We'd have a table of posh food for all our guests, then we'd have a table of pizza, chips, chicken wings and other junk for us! The walls would be made out of Häagen-Dazs Cookies and Cream ice-cream. When people arrived they'd get a spoon, and they could help themselves to the walls – dig in!

music Backstreet Boys, party music, anything you can dance to!

toast To success! To the fans who have supported us and everybody else who has helped us, happy New Year!

The walls would be made out of Häagen-Dazs Cookies and Cream ice-cream

Peter Wilby

guests Karl Marx To ask if he can explain where it all went wrong.
Clem Attlee To find out what he thinks of Tony Blair.
George Orwell To settle, once and for all, whether he would now be New Labour.
Oliver Cromwell To witness his amazement that the monarchy is still around.
Elizabeth I To hear her opinions of Margaret Thatcher.
J.F. Kennedy To see if he would seduce even the Virgin Queen next to him.
Emily Pankhurst To find out how militantly feminist she would seem now.
Marilyn Monroe To find out who really killed her.
Dorothy Parker To ensure there were some good jokes.
Jane Austen To raise the tone.
Sandra Wilby Because…well, she's my wife!

location The restaurant at the Sydney Opera House because it is the most romantic location in the world and would give the resurrected guests an idea of the late 20th century.

menu Champagne, strawberries and oysters only – everybody will be too busy talking to eat much.

music Beethoven's Symphony No.9

toast The old Millennium was dominated by war, superstition, injustice, massacre, disease, religion, waste, intolerance and ignorance. Even in its death throes it showed few signs of mending its ways. We can only toast a handful of great figures: Michelangelo; Leonardo da Vinci; Voltaire; Mozart; Beethoven; Picasso; Shakespeare; Tolstoy; Mark Twain; Einstein; Bertrand Russell; Darwin, and a few more who have added to human happiness, wisdom and enlightenment.
We should toast the survival of their values and insights into the next Millennium.

Norman Wisdom

I'm a lucky little devil!

guests Well, I wouldn't have Jesus as he'd have me chucked out! I'd have people I've met in my lifetime...

Charlie Chaplin A very nice fellow.

Edward G. Robinson Film actor – a bit of an old timer, from the gangster films.

Burt Lancaster Again, a very nice fellow.

Joan Crawford She was special. A marvellous actress...and there's a story behind this... I walked from London to Cardiff at 13, got a job as a cabin boy, travelled to the Argentine (it was great), and when I came back, I was scrounging for food at 3.30am at Victoria Station. This man said, 'Why don't you join the army?' I thought I was too young, but he told me that you could get into the band at 14. I said, 'But I don't know anything about music!', 'Kid them', he said. I put on the best act of my life. Anyhow, I had to hang about for two weeks before I could start, so I got a temporary job at Marble Arch Pavillion (now called the Odeon). I was operating the lift, and Joan Crawford got in. As we were going up to the first floor, she bent over and kissed me and rufffled my hair...which was lovely. Years later, when I was in Hollywood at a showbusiness lunch,

I told Joan Crawford the story. She remembered going up there in the lift and remembered that little boy. For the rest of the meal, we both ate with one hand each... we were holding each other's hand under the table.

Winston Churchill, Montgomery and Eisenhower It was wonderful to meet them. It was at the El Alamein reunion at Earls Court, donkeys years ago. All the troops there, including the US troops, and I did a show, and afterwards I met the three blokes – Winston, Monty, and Eisenhower.

Cassius Clay I met him years ago – a very nice man.

Mahatma Gandhi I met him, only for a minute or two...and to tell you the truth, I knew nothing about the business he was on about, but it was nice to meet him.

Liberace A really nice man, very down to earth.

Richard Rodgers Now there's a good story behind this one...

I was doing a show on Broadway, *Walking Happy*. After the show, this man says to me, 'I just saw your show'. I thought he was after an autograph and I thanked him. Then he says that he's putting on a show and he

wanted me to be in it – *Androcles and the Lion* – I definitely thought he was kidding, as there was no way anyone would want me to be in that play. 'Who else?', I asked. 'Noel Coward', he says. I was about to show him the door when he introduces himself to me as Richard Rodgers...and I ended up in his show.

location The canteen at Cheltenham barracks – it was where I was based in the War Office Signals. It would be lovely to do it there, with all the boys, at a reunion.

menu Shepherd's pie and butter beans, a drop of sweet cider to drink, and Ambrosia rice for pudding.

seating plan Me and Joan Crawford together...so we can hold hands.

music They could play *Don't Laugh at Me Because I'm a Fool* – my song!

toast I would propose a toast to all the friends who have helped me during my life to overcome my childhood, and get into a reasonabley successful career.

Well, I wouldn't have Jesus as he'd have me chucked out!

Mahatma Gandhi

Winston Churchill

Lewis Wolpert

A leading scientist who studies how embryos develop. More recently writing about the nature of depression – malignant sadness.

guests Archimedes First real scientist – applied maths to physical world.

Galileo Thought Archimedes wonderful; called him divine.

Faraday We could tell him what electricity has done. Very religious.

Shakespeare Because he is a wonderful genius. Nice for him to meet Hamlet.

Dr. S.Bremmer Because he is the wittiest scientist I know – a molecular biologist

Rory Bremner A genius comedian and mimic.

Madame Curie For her story of her discovery of radium.

Daniel Hume The only philosopher I really like.

Rosalind Franklin To tell her what has happened with her contribution to DNA.

Hamlet I would like to discuss his depression with him. Also he can meet his maker, Shakespeare.

Thomas Aquinas Good on religion and science.

location The Royal Society in London.

menu Only genetically modified foods where possible, to show confidence in that technology.

music Haydn, *The Creation*, seems appropriate.

toast To science – it has, in the old Millennium, proved to be the best way to understand how the world works. It has shown that the world works in ways that does not fit in with common sense. It has given us wonderful new technologies. In the new Millennium it will open up new vistas on the mind, in particular; and biology, in general. May the public learn to distinguish science from its applications and appreciate the power and value of its methods.

Ian Woosnam

Golfer. Since turning professional in 1976 Ian Woosnam has been a member of seven Ryder Cup Teams and has taken part in eleven World Cups. He won the 1997 Volvo European PGA Championship.

guests

Glen, my wife
Tom Jones
Shirley Bassey
Max Boyce
Ian Botham

Tommy Cooper
Whitney Houston
Muhammad Ali
Christy O'Connor
Tina Turner
Nicole Kidman

location Augusta – the site of my first major win.

music Tina Turner, *Simply the Best*.

toast I don't want to bore everyone so let's get on with the party.

World War I Veterans

James Hudson

guests **Jesus** He must be the guest of honour.

Mum and Dad Blessed with a very good memory, I recall many events in my first 18 months...seeing a troop train, believing the soldiers were waving and raising their bottles to me, to be told later by mum that I was, at that moment, taken off her hands and was in the care of her young teenage sister! Later, on Dad's shoulder, watching a firework display on Wish Tower Hill, Eastbourne, learning later that it was part of a ceremony celebrating The Relief of Mafeking. I can recall many family and domestic events and the strong family affection, so must seek the return of Mum and Dad.

Syd Hickmott Dear friend of my early teens. We found ourselves in World War I in separate battalions of the Queen's Own Royal West Kent Regiment. Syd was wounded and in a casualty clearing station which was shelled and, tragically, he was never seen again.

Bertie Blount CB Scientist, who, despite his strong animus against Hitler, became unpopular with those who, after the war, still wanted to grind Germany into dust. 'No' he said 'The war is over. Let's see what we can do in peace-time to help Germany to become a good democracy.'

Norman Lester Rowe CBE Skilled in oral and maxillofacial surgeon.

Dr. Findlater DSO (physician) Persuaded the Board to buy land, build a hospital, equip it and staff it with salaried specialists – the Redhill Hospital became the prototype for hospitals.

John Deacon MC Medical Officer in battalion of Naval Division.

Dr. David Barnard TDSRCS and **Dr. John L Williams** Worked very hard for the establishment of the new speciality of oral and maxillofacial surgery in the NHS hospital service.

Adelaide and **Valerie** Adelaide...dear sweetheart for 74 years; married 68. Nearly 93 at her Farewell. A tower of strength. Patiently waiting through my student years and gave up an operatic life. Her oustanding beautiful mezzo soprano voice a big loss to opera. With our lovely daughter, Valerie, they must be present.

Peter Firmston-Williams CB Seconded MI6.

Brian Hatton

Martyn Pedrick Friends and club members to teach a centenarian how to play putting clock golf..

Tony Parsons A delightful friend.

Peter Ustinov [host] To entertain.

menu I would like the menu of the luncheon on the occasion of being presented with the award of the Legion d'Honeur. The greatness and generosity of spirit which encouraged the government of France to extend such great honour to British as well as French survivors of the 14/18 campaign, was much appreciated.

location The Mansion, Moor Park Golf Club, Rickmansworth, Hertfordshire. Stately home with an interesting history.

toast To Friendship - that is my theme for this evening. To Friendship between all nations - in its complete meaning of civilisation.

Hal Kerridge

guests **Sir Winston Churchill** He was a man after my own heart.. a true Brit.

toast You can't turn back the clock, but if you could, well, I wonder whether you could bring back the simple, pure and honest sense of family that existed 50 or 60 years ago... that would do a world of good.

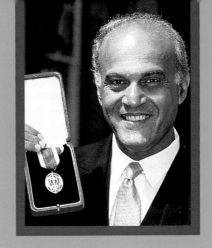

Sir Magdi Yacoub is a heart surgeon.

Magdi Yacoub

Marilyn Monroe

J.S. Bach

Galileo

guests J.S.Bach I find him intriguing, with an infinite creative capacity and the ability to achieve perfection in a predictable way.
Mahatma Gandhi For his courage, clear thinking and charismatic character.
Diana, Princess of Wales For her incredible vivaciousness, wit, deep thinking and compassion.
Sir Peter Medawar For his ability to combine science and philosophy and the capacity to articulate his thoughts in a clear fashion.
Bob Marley For his original style of music and philosophy.
Galileo For his pioneering work in science and thinking, in particular.
Sir Karl Popper For his optimistic outlook in interpreting evolution in general, and science and thinking, in particular.
Marilyn Monroe For her ability to influence people in a timeless fashion.
William Osler For his high morals and teachings in medicine, but also on life in general.

Che Guevara For the defiant insistence to project his ideas in a fearless fashion.
Mikhail Gorbachev For his incredible personality and the impact he had on the world.

location On a boat sailing down the Amazon.

menu Barbecued fish and vegetables. Rum cocktails (not sweet), followed by Baron de L white wine.

music
J.S.Bach: Well tempered clavier, *Book I*; *Tocata and Fugue* in D
Mozart: *Horn concerto*
Handel: *Zadok the priest*
Bob Marley: *No Woman, No Cry*
Mozart: *Requiem Lacupinosa*.
Handel: *Messiah - The Trumpet Shall Sound*

toast To the indefatigable creative human spirit.

To the indefatigable creative human spirit

and last but not least,

Captain Pugwash
(by John Ryan)

guests King Neptune • Christopher Columbus • Captain Cook • Long John Silver • Cut Throat Jake

location On board the "Black Pig".

music Handel's Water Music, played by cabin boy Tom on the concertina.

toast To all kids who want to be PIRATES!

Mr Benn
(by David McKee)

I have featured in books since 1967, and films since 1970. My adventures always started in a costume shop, by way of its changing room.

location Through the changing room of the costume shop and the second door that can lead to anywhere.

Paddington Bear
(by Michael Bond)

guests Paul Bocuse A very famous French chef... he has a recipe for marmalade pudding.
Francisco Pizarro He conquered Peru in 1530, so he should know some very good restaurants if I ever go back there.
Sir Isaac Newton It must be nice to have an apple fall on your head and discover gravity. I once had a fall on my head and all I discovered was a bruise.
Rebecca Price's mother One of the very first people in England to write down a recipe for orange marmalade.
Andre Previn
Jimmy Tarbuck He makes me laugh and he's a nice size – a bit like a bear.
Sherlock Holmes He could tell us about some of his favourite cases.
Bill Gates ...he seems to have practically invented computers, he ought to be around in case any go wrong on New Year's Eve.
Rory Bremner If any of the guests don't turn up he could impersonate them.
David Bailey He could take pictures of all the guests.
Mr.Gruber My best friend. Cyrano De Bergerac Chosen by Mr Nosy.
Road Runner Chosen by Mr Rush.
Walter Mitty Chosen by Mr Daydream.
Ken Dodd Chosen by Mr Tickle.

Mr Men
(by Adam Hargreaves)

guests   Einstein Chosen by Mr Clever.
Jackson Pollock Chosen by Mr Messy.
Obelix Chosen by Mr Strong.
Mona Lisa Chosen by Mr Happy.
Alexander Graham Bell Chosen by Mr. Chatterbox.
Scrooge Chosen by Mr Mean.

toast

'Happy Christmas!'
said Mr Muddle

Where's Wally?
(by Martin Handford)

My fantastic adventures have
been chronicled in books, magazines,
games and videos all over the world.
Wherever I go my faithful dog Woof is
never far from me.

My wish for the next Millennium is that man, using his intellect and
imagination, will make the world better for humans, nature and the
environment.
                                    Where's Wally © 1999. Martin Handford

Postman Pat
(by John Cuncliffe)

I'm the Greendale postman. I deliver the letters no matter what
happens; flood or frost, I'll get through.

toast

Keep the letters
coming!

The Wombles
(by Elizabeth Beresford)

location   The Womble's Feast will, of course, be held on
Wimbledon Common.

music   They will listen to Bungo's string band playing
Womble hits.

toast   Great Uncle Bulgaria will toast Wombles worldwide and
will express the hope that human beings will clear up after
themselves once the fantasy feasts are finished.

The Ultimate Last Supper

Jimi Hendrix

Frank Sinatra

Robbie Williams

Aretha Franklin

guest

Jesus Christ
William Shakespeare
Cleopatra
Marilyn Monroe
Oscar Wilde
Nelson Mandela
Elizabeth I
Billy Connolly
Muhammad Ali
Winston Churchill
Elvis Presley
Gandhi

music

The Beatles
Jimi Hendrix
Frank Sinatra
Mozart
Van Morrison
Robbie Williams' *Millennium*
Aretha Franklin
Handel's *Water Music*

food and drink

Champagne
Beer, Guinness
Château d'Yquem, Château
Lafite, Château Petrus,
Château Montrachet
Seafood
Beef on the bone
Sausages and mash
Foie gras
Caviar

destination

Home
Venice
Stonehenge
Table Mountain, South Africa
The Millennium Dome

Elizabeth I

Billy Connelly

Muhammad Ali

Elvis Presley

our hosts' favourite guests

Jesus Christ

Marilyn Monroe

Oscar Wilde

Nelson Mandela

guest **Jesus Christ**

'I need some answers.' – James Herbert

'It's his birthday.' – Marian Keyes

'To discover the truth, once and for all.' – Maggie Koumi

'He would approve of saving the children.' – Christopher Martin Jenkins

'It is his 2000th, so it would be rude not to invite him.' – Chris Moon

'So as he could turn water into Malibu and coke.' – San and Tray (Viz)

'I wouldn't have Jesus as he'd have me chucked out!' – Norman Wisdom

William Shakespeare

'To tell us a little about his life and dreams.' – Tony Bullimore

'For his after dinner stories.' – William Hague

'So I can teach him how to spell.' – Piers Morgan

Cleopatra

'The first feminist.' – David Bailey.

Marilyn Monroe

'For fun.' – Ronnie Barker

'Because gentlemen prefer... ' – Terence Conran

'To sing 'Happy Birthday' to the Millennium.' – Bill Emmott

'For that necessary touch of glamour.' – Dave Gaskill

'The sexiest woman who ever lived.' – Ozzy Osbourne

'To find out who really killed her.' – Peter Wilby

Oscar Wilde

'For wit.' – George Best

'A supreme story teller.' – Joan Collins

'Great wit and raconteur.' - Clarissa Dickson Wright

'(his) wit (drier than an AA clinic) should have been registered at police headquarters as a lethal weapon.' – Kathy Lette

Nelson Mandela

'For his humanity and great wisdom.' – Peter Ustinov

'Who needs a reason?' – Glenda Jackson

Elizabeth I 'For greatness.' Ronnie Barker.

'The virgin Queen of England, whose reign gave birth to a renaissance.' – Benazir Bhutto.

'Lady with an attitude.' – Sister Bliss.

'To hear her opinions of Margaret Thatcher.' – Peter Wilby.

Billy Connolly

'The funniest man alive.' – Mr Blobby

'For the comedy.' – Garin Jenkins.

'Because he is a friend and a great conversationalist.' – Jackie Stewart.

Muhammad Ali

'Total hero' – Another Level

'So no one else on the table can be the greatest.' – Michael Barrymore

'The greatest fighter.' – Tony Parsons

'He's just a legend.' – Iwan Thomas

Winston Churchill

'To have a drink with him. –

George Best.

'I been moved to tears when reading some of his speeches. His use of English defies description.' – John Elkington.

'My personal hero.' – Sir Ranulph Fiennes.

'Because he is what Britain should be all about.' – Piers Morgan.

Elvis Presley

'To give us a little song.' – Declan Donnolly

'Those looks, those hips, that voice.' Caroline Crumby

'Love the way he moves.' – Kelly Hoppen

'The King.' – Julian Lloyd-Webber

'Rock 'n' roll hero.' – Irvine Welsh

Mahatma Gandhi

'Violence is our curse, Gandhi its enemy.' – Sir Ranulph Fiennes.

'The bravest spiritual leader of the century.' – Adam Rickitt.

'For his courage, clear thinking and charismatic character.' – Magdi Yacoub

Credits

Page 6 © Penny Tweedie (left and middle) for Save the Children © Caroline Penn for Save the Children. **Page 7** Princess Anne © Fritz Curzon for Save the Children. **Page 9** A1© Mark Allen, ALPHA. Robbie Williams © Jeff Walker, FAMOUS. **Page 10** All Saints © Dave Morgan, ALPHA. Brad Pitt © Rob Howard, FAMOUS. Sesame Street © ALPHA. **Page 11** David Bowie© Hubert Boesl, FAMOUS. Frank Sinatra © Corbis/Bettmann. Page 12 Ant and Dec© Fred Duval, FAMOUS. Eddie Izzard © Ashley Knutek, ALPHA. Basil Brush © Boom Boom Ltd. Another Level, Mark Baron. **Page 13** Anthony McPartlin © Jeff Spicer, ALPHA. Jack Nicholson © Kurt Krieger, FAMOUS. John Lennon © Corbis/S.I.N. **Page 14** Houdini © Corbis. **Page 15** Jeffrey Archer © Jeff Spicer, ALPHA. Thomas Jefferson © The Mary Evans Picture Library. Nelson Mandela © Steve Finn, ALPHA. Benjamin Disraeli © The Illustrated London News Picture Library. Elizabeth I © The Illustrated London News Picture Library. **Page 16** Paddy Ashdown © Robin Price, ALPHA. Tasmin Archer © Ian Dickson, ALPHA. **Page 17** Lao Tse © Mary Evans Picture Library. **Page 18** Naim Attallah © Riccardo Pavoncelli. **Page 19** David Bailey © Ashley Knotek, ALPHA. Orson Welles © Corbis/Hulton Deutsch. Louis Armstrong © Corbis/Bettmann. Pablo Picasso © ALPHA/S&G. **Page 20** Ronnie Barker © Dave Benett, ALPHA. Danny Kaye © ALPHA/SPORT & GENERAL. Dorothy Parker © Corbis/Bettmann. Orson Welles © Corbis/Hulton Deutsch. **Page 21** Michael Barrymore © Brian Moody, Scope Features. Jack Nicholson © Hubert Boesl, FAMOUS. Princess Diana © Fred Duval, FAMOUS. Joanna Lumley © Jeff Walker, FAMOUS. Oprah Winfrey © Hubert Boesl, FAMOUS. **Page 22** Basil Brush © Boom Boom Ltd. David Attenborough © Corbis. **Page 23** George Best © Corbis/Hulton Deutsch. Rod Stewart © Hubert Boesl/FAMOUS. Elizabeth Taylor © Corbis/Bettmann. Sir Winston Churchill © The Illustrated London News Picture Library. Brigitte Bardot © Corbis/Bettmann. **Page 24** Betty Boop © ALPHA. Madonna © ALPHA. Gabrielle Chanel © Corbis/Underwood & Underwood. Marilyn Monroe© ALPHA. **Page 26** Raymond Blanc © Richard Chambury, ALPHA. **Page 27** Oscar Wilde © The Illustrated London News Picture Library. Germaine Greer © Richard Chambury, ALPHA. Liz Taylor and Richard Burton © Corbis/Bettmann. **Page 28** Boy George © Chris Clunn. Tom Cruise © Hubert Boesl, FAMOUS. The Dalai Lama © Richard Chambury, ALPHA. David Bowie © Hubert Boesl, FAMOUS. David Beckham © Fred Duval, FAMOUS. **Page 29** Jo Brand © Richard Chambury, ALPHA. Germaine Greer © Richard Chambury, ALPHA. Mary Wollstonecraft © Mary Evans Picture Library. Jesus © Mary Evans Picture Library. **Page 30** Brad Pitt © Rob Howard, FAMOUS. Harrison Ford © Hubert Boesl, FAMOUS. David Ginola © Fred Duval, FAMOUS. George Clooney © Kurt Krieger, FAMOUS. **Page 31** Kelly Brook © Fred Duval, FAMOUS. David Niven © Corbis/Hulton Deutsch. Oscar Wilde © The Illustrated London News Picture Library. Elizabeth I © The Illustrated London News Picture Library. **Page 32** Gordon Brown © P. Aitchison, ALPHA. Nelson Mandela © ALPHA. Martin Luther King © The Illustrated London News Picture Library. J.S. Bach © Mary Evans Picture Library. Jessye Norman © Richard Chambury, ALPHA. **Page 33** Julie Burchill © Mark Guthrir. Josef Stalin © Hulton Deutsch. Will Self © Richard Chambury, ALPHA. **Page 34** Tony Bullimore © Jeff Spicer, ALPHA. **Page 35** Darcy Bussell © Dave Benett, ALPHA. Elvis Presley © ALPHA. Fred Astaire © Corbis/Bettmann. Sean Connery © Corbis/Bettmann. Audrey Hepburn © Corbis/Underwood & Underwood. **Page 36** The Queen Mother © S.D.Newton, FAMOUS. Hillary Clinton © Mark Young, FAMOUS. **Page 37** Ffyona Campbell © Steve Finn, ALPHA. **Page 38** Will Carling © Steve Finn, ALPHA. Jacqueline Bisset © Delmas, FAMOUS. Eddie Izzard © Fred Duval, FAMOUS. Robin Williams © Hubert Boesl, FAMOUS. **Page 39** Anna Carteret © Peter Aitchison, ALPHA. Maya Angelou © ALPHA. Elvis Presley © ALPHA. Danny Kaye © ALPHA/SPORT & GENERAL. **Page 40** Christopher Chataway © ALPHA. **Page 41** The Chemical Brothers © Felipe, FAMOUS. Muhammad Ali © ALPHA. **Page 42** Joan Collins © Jeff Walker, FAMOUS. Marlene Dietrich © Corbis/Bettmann. **Page 43** Terence Conran © Jeff Spicer, ALPHA. Marilyn Monroe © ALPHA. **Page 44** Henry Cooper © Richard Chambury, ALPHA. **Page 45** Jilly

Cooper © Bob Langrish. Jesus © Mary Evans Picture Library. The apostles © Mary Evans Picture Library. Saint Andrew © Mary Evans Picture Library. **Page 46** David Beckham © Fred Duval, FAMOUS. Joanna Lumley © Jeff Walker, FAMOUS. Prince William © Dave Chancellor, ALPHA. Madonna © Kurt Krieger, FAMOUS. **Page 47** The Cranberries © Kyran O'Brian, ALPHA. Sean Connery © ALPHA. Robert de Niro © Kurt Krieger, FAMOUS. Elvis Presley © ALPHA. **Page 48** Steve Elworthy © M. Haroun, ALPHA. Jacques Kallis © Karwai Tang, ALPHA. Sandra Bullock © AUTA, FAMOUS. **Page 49** Brad Pitt © Rob Howard, FAMOUS. **Page 50** Steven Spielberg © Kurt Krieger, FAMOUS. Jennifer Aniston © ALPHA. Harrison Ford © Hubert Boesl, FAMOUS. **Page 51** Lara Croft © Core Design 4D 1999. **Page 52** Elvis Presley © ALPHA. **Page 54** Laura Davies © ALPHA. Michael Jordan © Hubert Boesl, FAMOUS. **Page 55** Christopher Dean © ALPHA. Audrey Hepburn © Corbis/Underwood & Underwood. Fred Astaire © Corbis/Bettmann. Ian Botham © ALPHA. Princess Diana © Alan Towse, FAMOUS. **Page 57** Sean Bean © Hubert Boesl, FAMOUS. Arnold Schwarzenegger © Hubert Boesl, FAMOUS. **Page 58** Charles II © Mary Evans Picture Library. Oscar Wilde © The Illustrated London News Picture Library. Saint Teresa © Mary Evans Picture Library. **Page 59** Lee Dixon © R. Pelham, ALPHA. **Page 60** Adolf Hitler © The Illustrated London News Picture Library. Anne Frank © Corbis/Bettmann. Leon Greenman © Corbis/Howard Davies. Heinrich Himmler© The Illustrated London News Picture Library. **Page 64** Houdini © Corbis. **Page 65** J.R.R.Tolkien © Corbis/Bettmann. James Cook © Mary Evans Picture Library. Mahomet © Mary Evans Picture Library. Ptolemy © Mary Evans Picture Library. **Page 66** Sherlock Holmes & Dr Watson © Hulton Getty. Bob Dylan © ALPHA. **Page 67** Steve McQueen © Corbis/Bettman. John Lennon © Corbis/S. I. N. J. R .R. Tolkien © Corbis/Bettmann. **Page 68** Emma Forbes © Steve Finn, ALPHA. Jerry Seinfeld © Hubert Boesl, FAMOUS. Jerry Springer © Hubert Boesl, FAMOUS. Billy Connolly © Hubert Boesl, FAMOUS. Kim Basinger © Hubert Boesl, FAMOUS. **Page 69** Bella Freud © Steve Finn, ALPHA. Mae West © Corbis/Bettmann. Colette © Mary Evans Picture Library. Leonard Cohen © Corbis. **Page 71** Uri Geller © Alan Towse, FAMOUS. Albert Einstein © The Illustrated London News Picture Library. Sigmund Freud © The Illustrated London News Picture Library. Carl Jung © Mary Evans Picture Library. **Page72** Gene © Andrew Carruth, FAMOUS. Dorothy Parker © Corbis/Bettmann. Mozart © Corbis. Jacqueline du Pre © Corbis/Hulton Deutsch. Madonna © Kurt Kreiger, FAMOUS. **Page 73** Lord Gowrie © Richard Chambury, ALPHA. **Page 74** Graham Gooch © Steve Finn, ALPHA. Pele © Ashley Knotek, ALPHA. Rowan Atkinson © Paul Lovelace, FAMOUS. Susan Greenfield © Steve Finn, ALPHA. Albert Einstein © The Illustrated London News Picture Library. Elizabeth I © The Illustrated London News Picture Library. **Page 76** Eric Hall © Karwai Tang, ALPHA. Frank Sinatra © Corbis/Bettmann. **Page 77** William Hague © Steve Finn, ALPHA. The Beatles © Corbis/Bettmann. William Shakespeare © Hulton Getty. Elizabeth I © The Illustrated London News Picture Library. **Page 78** Michael Jordan © Hubert Boesl, FAMOUS. Muhammad Ali © ALPHA. **Page 79** Nick Hancock © Ashley Knotek, ALPHA. Happy Mondays © ALPHA. Jesus © Mary Evans Picture Library. **Page 80** Wayne Hemmingway © Morley von Sternberg. Gordon Banks © Ahsley Knotek, ALPHA. Bobby Moore © Karwai Tang, ALPHA. Bobby Charlton © Steve Finn, ALPHA. **Page 81** H.G.Wells © Mary Evans Picture Library. John F. Kennedy © Mary Evans Picture Library. Steve McQueen © Corbis/Bettmann. Brigitte Bardot © Corbis/Bettmann. **Page 83** Christopher Hibbert © Ellen Warner. Harold Pinter © Dave Benett, ALPHA. Joan Collins © Fred Duval, FAMOUS. **Page 84** Andy Hinchliffe © Magi Haroun, ALPHA. John Major © Fred Duval, FAMOUS. Liam Gallagher © Fred Duval, FAMOUS. Quentin Tarantino © FAMOUS. **Page 85** Lloyd Honeyghan. The Honeyz © Richard Chambury, ALPHA. Mariah Carey © Hubert Boesl, FAMOUS. Marilyn Monroe © ALPHA. William Shakespeare © Hulton Getty. **Page 86** Kelly Hoppen © D. Benett, ALPHA. Pablo Picasso © ALPHA. Richard Gere © Atva, FAMOUS. The Dalai Lama © Richard Chambury, ALPHA. **Page 87** Barry Humphries © R. Pelham, ALPHA. **Page 88** Will Hutton © Jane Brown. Van Morrison © Corbis/Neal Preston. Adam Smith © Mary Evans Picture Library. Marilyn Monroe © ALPHA. **Page 89** Glenda Jackson © Jeff Spicer, ALPHA. Marlon Brando © ALPHA. Fred Astaire ©

Thank you

If you're like me, this is the part of a book that you normally just skip over...which is a shame because *Fantasy Feast 2000* simply could not have been produced without the help, advice, time and money given to us by this virtual directory of people and companies. So if you've got a moment, please have a look - these people deserve your acknowledgement.

Media & Celebrity Listings
These companies have helped us
put together a contact book to die
for. We owe you big!
The Profile Group
   (inc. Entertainment News) – sorry
   for all the extra requests Sara.
London At Large
PiMS
Spotlight
Pollstar UK
Music Week Publishing

Celebrity agents &
contacts
Without you, we wouldn't have had
the chance to get many of the
contributors to write about their
Fantasy Feasts.
Amnesty International
Ant & Dec Productions
Association of Illustrators
Aston Villa FC
Automatic Management
Avalon Management
Bacchus
Barry Collings Entertainment
BBC Children's Publishing
BBC Worldwide
Billy Marsh Associates
Bloomsbury Publishing
Boom Boom
Capersville
Cartoon Network
Cheeky Records
Children's TV Workshop
Chorion plc

Christians in Sport
Colin Rushton
Collins Willow
Commission for Racial Equality
Conservative Central Office
Core Design
Crystal Palace FC
Cue Masters
Curtis Brown Agency
D.E.F. Management
David Higham Associates
Deborah McKenna
ECB
Ed Victor Agency
Eidos
EMI
Everton FC
Federation Francaise de Rugby
First Avenue Entertainment
First Column Management
Freud Communications
Freya Miller Agency
Friends of the Earth
Furtive Management
Gillon Aitken Associates
Granta Publications
Greenpeace
Hamlyn – you taught me all I
   needed to know about
   publishing! You gave me the
   determination to make this work.
   I hope you like it!
HarperCollins
Harrods
Hazemead
Hello!
Hit Entertainment

Hodder Children's Books
ICM
IMG – Artists
IMG – Sport
IRFU
James Grant Management
Jim Henson Productions
John Brown Publishers
Jonathan Cape Publishers
King Features Syndicate
King Rollo Films
Knight Ayton Management
Left Bank Management
Link Licensing
Living TV
London News Radio
London Records
London Weekend Television
Macmillan Books
Mattell
Media Machine
Megan Willis
Megastar Productions
Mel Bush Organisation
Mercury Records
Mersey TV
Michael O'Mara Books
Middlesbrough FC
National Council of Hindu
Temples
New Zealand Cricket Board
Off the Kerb Promotions
Orion Books
Oxford University Press
Paul Smith
PBJ Management
Penguin Books

Personal Appearances
Peters, Fraser & Dunlop
Polydor Records
Press Counsel
Primary
Public Image
Quartet Books
Random House
Red Rooster
Reprasentz
Robert Smith Literary Agents
Royal Opera House
Sharon Osbourne Management
Sheffield Wednesday FC
Sixuvus Management
SJM
Smash Hits
SNP
Sooty Enterprises
Soul 2Soul
Southampton FC
Stan Green Ltd
Steve Kuttner
Testimony Films
The Beano
The Cartoon Club of Great Britain
The Copyright Company
The Dandy
The Economist
The Evening Standard
The Hargreaves Organisation
The Liberal Democrats
The Licensing Company
The Mirror
The National Autistic Society
The New Statesman
The Observer

The Pagan Federation

The Royal Opera House

The Sun

The Wright Publicity

Tony Davis Management

Tony Denton Promotions

Trouble TV

UK Athletics

Unique Group

United Cricket Board of South Africa

Viz

Walker Books

Watford FC

Wildlife Entertainment

Wise Buddah

WRU

WWF

The A list

There are a number of people who really have had to suffer. To the following, thanks of even greater enormity is due…

Alex Proud – who is usually single, largely eligible and owns the best photographic gallery in London. Number available on request.

Johnny Weir – The Angst will soon be over..

Vanessa Hogg & Colin Hogg DL

Adrian Bignell

Alexi Rosin

Alex Wooff

Alison at Cue Masters

Alistair Wanklyn

Andrew Whitelam at Superleague Europe

Anouschka Menzies at Bacchus

Ben Scott

Ben Weston

Betty Swallocks

Catherine Whitty

Cheriff Riffaat

Claire Gilmour at Steve Kuttner

Claire Pilcher

Colin Rushton

Elaine Westbrook at Freud Communications

Emmy Osher

Claire, Rebecca, Richard, Sacha & Simone at Slice PR – the best publicity outfit in the UK!

Gareth Collett

Getty Images - About the first company to back us. Thanks Jo!

Imran Khan

Jacquie Morel

James Cranmer – and you also got married!

James Hopkins

Jane Wright at The Wright Publicity

Jeremy Singer at M&M

Jim 'fingers' Whyte – yer still yella!

John Knight at Ant & Dec

John Mckie at Smash Hits

Jon Lewis

Katie Crichton-Miller

Karen Brown

Laura Barclay

Lorna Carmichael

Louise Wanless at Middlesbrough FC – you're brilliant!

Lucy Barber

Mark Worthington

Mel Thomas at London Records – I can't believe you never gave up on us!

Ned Whitley

Nick Dewey at the Chemical Brothers office

Nick Duffy

Nicola Loud at Mercury Records

Nicollette Dawson

Nikki March

Ollie Hendrie at The Box Patrick and Peter de Vink

Penny at Lichfield Studios

Phil Day

Phil Hughes

Rebeca Marton

Red Snapper – for the top quality design & print of our press materials.

Richard Hoftstetter

Richard Van Emden at Testimony Films

Rob Hierons

Rosie Corcoran

Sam Field

Greta Sani

Simon & Schuster

Simon Willis at Conran Holdings – I'm sorry..

Stephanie Hardwick from BBC Radio 2 Publicity

Sue Young

Suzy Lambert

Suzy Pilcher

Terence Parris

Thomas Jenkins

Tim Wooff

Trevor James at WRU

…and to all the others who've helped us and we've forgotten to name here: we're as grateful as we are forgetful – THANKS!

The idea

Finally a word of thanks to Adam Rattray and Mr Bushby (my old History teacher) for inspiring the concept behind Fantasy Feast. It is almost exactly ten years ago that we spent the end of an A Level history lesson discussing which historical characters we would like to meet. My memory is worryingly vague, but I'm pretty sure that, on Adam's suggestion, Mr Bushby put aside the end of a lesson to discuss the idea. It clearly had a big impression on me…many thanks! (For the record, Adam would like to stress that he got the idea from a magazine article.).

Hector Proud

Hector Proud

Hector Proud was born in Brighton in 1971. Having studied History at St Andrews University, he worked for three years in environmental public relations, leaving his job in Spring 1998 to develop the Fantasy Feast 2000 project.

He is now Director of Idea Generation, a project management company established for *Fantasy Feast 2000*, with a view to producing other similar projects of an altruistic nature in the future.

He works with his brother Alex at The Proud Galleries next to the Strand, London.

The *Fantasy Feast 2000* concept was developed by Hector Proud and The Idea Generation Company to raise funds for Save The Children. All author royalties are being donated to Save the Children.

A special thank you

Thanks to all at Everyman, and Biljana and Kicca at bk design.

192